THE HOMEMADE *Pie* COOKBOOK

100 Pie, Tart, and Galette Recipes for Every Season

LAURA KLYNSTRA

THE HOMEMADE PIE

COOKBOOK

Revell

a division of Baker Publishing Group
Grand Rapids, Michigan

Text and photography © 2025 by Laura Klynstra

Published by Revell
a division of Baker Publishing Group
Grand Rapids, Michigan
RevellBooks.com

Printed in China

Library of Congress Cataloging-in-Publication Data
Names: Klynstra, Laura, author.
Title: The homemade pie cookbook : 100 pie, tart, and galette recipes for every season / Laura Klynstra.
Description: Grand Rapids, Michigan : Revell, a division of Baker Publishing Group, [2025] | Includes bibliographical references.
Identifiers: LCCN 2024053722 | ISBN 9780800747015 (cloth) | ISBN 9781493451500 (ebook)
Subjects: LCSH: Pies. | Desserts. | Baking. | LCGFT: Cookbooks.
Classification: LCC TX773 .K57445 2025 | DDC 641.86/52—dc23/eng/20250131
LC record available at https://lccn.loc.gov/2024053722

25 26 27 28 29 30 31   7 6 5 4 3 2 1

NOTE: Consuming raw or undercooked eggs may increase your risk of foodborne illness, and foods that contain raw eggs (or eggs that have not been heated to at least 160°F) should not be prepared for pregnant women, babies, young children, elderly persons, or anyone whose health is compromised.

Cover photograph by Laura Klynstra
Author photograph by Mehreen Jabbar

Baker Publishing Group publications use paper produced from sustainable forestry practices and postconsumer waste whenever possible.

For Joyce, who made the kitchen the heart of our home and who taught me that love can come served in a pie dish.

For Helene, who found joy in simple things and always hummed while she worked.

And for Lorraine, who carries family memories like treasures and always shows up in good times and tough times with fellowship, resilience, and grace.

Contents

SUMMER

Sweet Pies

Savory Pies

FALL

Sweet Pies

Savory Pies

WINTER

Sweet Pies

Savory Pies

GARNISHES AND TOPPINGS

Introduction

Like most kids who start baking early, cookies were *my thing* growing up, and I made a lot of them. Shortbreads with jam fillings, gooey chocolate brownie-like varieties, cinnamony snickerdoodles, and of course every variation of chocolate chip I could find. My mom made wedding cakes out of our home, so I had an unending supply of decorating tools, which I soon started using to decorate shaped cookies. It got to the point that cookies just *seemed* easy. Contrary to the saying *easy as pie*, pie did not.

Cakes were my mom's business but pies were her favorite, and she baked many. She hated rolling out dough, though, and always took the shortcut of buying premade crust. It wasn't until I had my own home kitchen that I started to tackle the craft of making homemade pies completely from scratch. Eventually, I found that pies *are* easy. They may take a little more time and dexterity than a simple drop cookie, but I realized if I gave myself time to make something by hand, it was not only doable but also relaxing. It gave space for my head to slow down a bit and just focus on creating something with my hands. I spent so much time at my computer designing things electronically—creating something tangible was rewarding, and it was so fun to see (and smell) the finished pies coming out of the oven. They weren't perfect, but they were still beauties.

When I worked in New York City, I would sometimes bring baked goods to the office. Since the city's buildings are filled mostly with commuters, homemade goodies were a rarity. There's very little joy in lugging a cake or pie onto the bus and then down the stairs of the subway and carrying it several blocks while dodging taxis. But I found that sharing them did bring joy—lots of it, both to my colleagues who thoroughly enjoyed having something special and fresh, and to me in knowing that something I created with my own hands and craft made someone else's day a little sweeter.

Pies have since become a favorite of mine, but I still enjoy all those cookie flavors from my childhood. I mix them into my pies whenever I can dream up a combination that will work. I usually save pie baking for special occasions: times of sharing, holiday meals, company potlucks, and dinner parties with old friends. Garnished with whipped cream or an eat-it-soon-before-it-melts scoop of ice cream, a steaming cup of dark roast coffee, and an agreeable conversation, pies are the sweet (or savory) center to many happy moments. Some of my best Thanksgiving memories revolve around tables filled with pie options so plentiful that someone inevitably pipes up, *I'll take a sliver of each!* Conversations while standing in the office hallway holding a plate of buttery, crumble-topped apple pie make colleagues more like friends.

Pies of endless varieties have worked their way into our celebrations and the special times of our lives, so much so that they hold a reverence that makes them anything but humble. Perhaps that's why I think of them as gifts or slices to be gathered around and shared. The very act of meticulously working cold butter into flour and molding crust to pie plate feels like a kind of love.

The craft and time that make pies so unique can also make them seem too difficult, like it's just too much to tackle. It's hard not to feel a little frustrated when the crust sticks to the rolling pin, or disappointed in an uneven crimp, or worried about the flour and crumbs

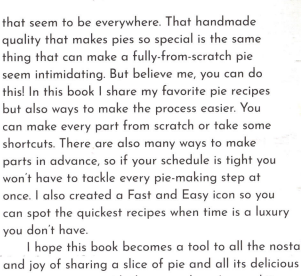

that seem to be everywhere. That handmade quality that makes pies so special is the same thing that can make a fully-from-scratch pie seem intimidating. But believe me, you can do this! In this book I share my favorite pie recipes but also ways to make the process easier. You can make every part from scratch or take some shortcuts. There are also many ways to make parts in advance, so if your schedule is tight you won't have to tackle every pie-making step at once. I also created a Fast and Easy icon so you can spot the quickest recipes when time is a luxury you don't have.

I hope this book becomes a tool to all the nostalgia and joy of sharing a slice of pie and all its delicious accompaniments with those you love. In good times and bad, pie will always make life a little sweeter and will make those sitting with you feel the love.

Ingredients

If you're afraid of butter, use cream.

—Julia Child

Before you begin baking, get your pantry and refrigerator stocked with these essential pie-baking ingredients. High-quality, fresh, and in-season ingredients make the most delicious pies. So always buy the best ingredients you can find.

BUTTER

Butter is an essential component of most pies, starting with the crust. There are vegan options, but for the most part, if you're eating pie, there's probably butter in it. I adore European butter, but for the sake of pie crust I lean more toward American butter, which has a lower amount of butterfat, making it harder when cold. The tendency of European butter to be softer and melt faster makes it more difficult to work with when trying to cut (not blend or cream) butter into flour for crust. You can certainly use European butter, which usually has a superior taste, but just know that you may need to stop working to cool your ingredients more often if using this higher butterfat version.

HEAVY CREAM

Perhaps not a common ingredient found in a typical refrigerator, heavy cream (or whipping cream) suddenly becomes a staple when making pies. Between homemade ice cream, whipped cream, and cold-set fillings, heavy cream is an essential ingredient. Skip the little pint and go for the larger container if multiple pies are on your agenda. The more natural varieties may have the cream rise to the top, so be sure to shake the container before opening

and check if any of the cream is stuck near the top before using.

EGGS

We raise chickens, and they produce the most amazing eggs. Birds that live natural lives as omnivores foraging on grass produce the best, most vitamin-rich eggs with a yolk that is closer to orange than yellow. If raising your own chickens is not your cup of tea, look for eggs from local producers of pasture-raised hens in your neighborhood or at farmers' markets. You can also purchase naturally raised eggs in most supermarkets. Look for "pasture-raised," which means the hens are outside in nature, versus "free range" or "cage-free," which usually means the hens are living in large pole barns.

Most recipes in this book call for room temperature eggs. This is to avoid having butter seize up from the cold temperature. If you forget to take your eggs out of the refrigerator on time, you can bring them to room temperature by placing them in a bowl of warm water for 10 minutes.

FLOUR

For pies and tarts, I recommend having both all-purpose and cake flour on hand. I use all-purpose flour for pie crusts and cake flour for tart crusts. The lower gluten content in cake flour makes for a more tender tart crust. The medium level of gluten in all-purpose flour gives better structure to pie dough for flakiness and strength.

Weighing is the best way to measure flour, since it can get packed into a measuring cup, resulting in too much flour. If you don't weigh your flour, the best practice is to first fluff it up and then scoop it into the measuring cup. Use the flat side of a butter knife to scrape off the extra.

FRUITS AND VEGETABLES

The recipes in this book are intended to make the best use of local harvests. Of course, not all fruits can be acquired from local farms, but when you can get in-season fresh fruits and vegetables, take advantage and bake something with them. They will bring out the best in your pies, tarts, and galettes.

CITRUS

Lemon juice and lime juice are used in many pie recipes in this book. It is best practice to use freshly squeezed citrus juice for a brighter, more pronounced flavor. Always use fresh zest when the recipe calls for it. If, in a pinch, you need to use dried zest, reduce the amount to one-third. Dried zest is more potent than fresh.

CORNSTARCH

Cornstarch is a thickening agent essential in many pie fillings. Though technically it doesn't go bad, I have noticed that older cornstarch can clump, causing problems when trying to work it into a recipe. If you see that your cornstarch is clumping, either pass it through a fine mesh sieve or throw it out and buy a fresh container. I like Bob's Red Mill brand best. For anyone allergic to cornstarch, arrowroot powder can be substituted at a 1-for-1 ratio.

UNFLAVORED GELATIN

I use unflavored gelatin in a few recipes as a way to achieve some of that nostalgic Jell-O style without any artificial flavors and colors. Regular gelatin is made from animal collagen, so be aware that any pie with gelatin is not vegan.

MAPLE SYRUP

The most essential thing to remember with maple syrup is to only use the real stuff. Look for *pure* on the label. Inexpensive syrups are usually corn syrup with artificial flavors and should never be used in recipes that call for maple syrup. The real thing is pricey but worth it. Select grade B for a darker syrup with richer flavor.

CHOCOLATE AND COCOA POWDER

When it comes to chocolate and cocoa powder, you get what you pay for. It really is worth the money to buy a higher quality. Higher quality chocolate tastes better and melts better, making it easier to work with. Valrhona makes excellent chocolate and unsweetened cocoa powder. Guittard is also a favorite brand of mine; with excellent flavor and fair-trade production, it is a great staple to keep in your pantry. When melting chocolate, it is best practice to use a coarsely chopped chocolate bar rather than chocolate chips.

There are three forms of cocoa powder: unsweetened (or natural) cocoa powder, Dutch process cocoa powder, and black cocoa powder. Unsweetened cocoa powder is the one most of us grew up using from the Hershey's can. If a recipe doesn't specify which cocoa powder to use, unsweetened is the go-to. Dutch process cocoa is less acidic and has a more mellow flavor. Black cocoa is even more processed than Dutch process cocoa, which further reduces the acidity. It has an ultra dark color and smooth texture, and it is responsible for much of the unique flavor of Oreo cookies. As with solid chocolate, flavor will also be influenced by the brand, and higher quality cocoas will bring the best taste to your finished pies.

VANILLA

Vanilla is the most essential extract to keep in your pantry. Pure vanilla extract is made from dried vanilla beans soaked in alcohol for months. Imitation vanilla is a chemically synthesized vanillin flavor—only one of vanilla's three hundred flavors. Real vanilla is complex and adds depth to every recipe. I use vanilla in three forms: extract, bean paste, and beans. Vanilla bean paste and beans have stronger flavor and will also add dark, tiny flecks to your baked pies. Buying vanilla beans individually is very pricey. If you bake a lot, purchase them in bulk and store in the refrigerator.

unsweetened cocoa

black cocoa

Dutch process cocoa

Equipment

STAND MIXER

If you are going to splurge on one small kitchen appliance, make it a stand mixer. I keep all of my small appliances tucked away for tidy counters, except for my stand mixer, which I use almost every day. From pie doughs to fillings to meringues, curds, and whipped creams—everything is easier with a stand mixer. I recommend also getting a pastry attachment and an extra metal bowl. Stand mixers make everything easier, but if you don't have one, a hand mixer works; it will just take a little more effort and attention.

ROLLING PINS AND PASTRY BOARDS

There are many rolling pin options out there. I've used many kinds, but my go-to is a simple wood rolling pin. If you have natural stone countertops, you already have the perfect surface to roll out dough. If you don't, a marble pastry board is great for rolling out pie dough. Marble is naturally cooler than other surfaces and helps keep butter cool while working with dough.

THERMOMETERS

Many ovens don't have accurate temperatures. Oven thermometers are inexpensive and can help ensure you are baking at the right temperature. Always keep in mind that because ovens differ, your bake times may also differ. Use the time on a recipe as a guide, but also use the visual cues I've indicated to decide whether your pie is ready. It is also helpful to have an instant read thermometer when making Swiss meringue, custards, and curds.

pastry attachment
for stand mixer

instant read thermometer

whisk attachment
for stand mixer

pastry board
and rolling pin

kitchen scissors

pastry bags
and tips

rolling pin

cookie
scoops

cherry
pitter

measuring
spoons

cookie cutters
and stamps

pastry brushes

kitchen
scale

pastry wheel

pre-cut parchment paper

fine mesh sieve

whisks

tart tamper

zester

masking tape and permanent marker

bench scraper

spouted saucepan

measuring cups

Made in France 521 Q19

pie weights

baking sheets and nonstick mats

PIE PLATES

My first pie plate was a red ceramic Emile Henry deep-dish. As I tried multiple pie recipes in my new pie plate, I started to wonder why the fillings seemed to only take up half of it. As it turns out, most pie recipes are written for a classic 9-inch pie plate, which is between 1 and 1½ inches tall. Deep-dish pie plates can be over 2½ inches tall and have nearly twice the volume of a classic pie plate. Many of the recipes in this book are scaled to fit a deep-dish pie plate. It is important to check the dish indicated for each recipe. This information will be in the text of the recipe and located on the recipe's label at the bottom of the page. You can always use a deep-dish pie plate instead of a classic pie plate, but if you try to fit a deep-dish recipe into a classic-sized plate, you could have problems.

Disposable pie plates are almost always meant for classic-sized pies. When gifting a deep-dish pie, be sure to look for a disposable dish that is at least 2 inches deep.

Other kinds of baking dishes used throughout the book include skillets, mini pie plates, springform pans, and half-sheet baking pans.

WHAT TO DO IF YOUR PIE PLATE IS TOO SMALL

The classic-sized pies in this book were tested in a pie plate with a 1-quart capacity, and the deep dish recipes were tested in a pie plate with a 3¼-quart capacity. Because pie plates vary, yours may be smaller than these. If the filling doesn't fit, simply add extra filling to a ramekin or mini pie plate and create a mini pie for the baker.

skillet

half-sheet baking sheet for slab pies

classic-sized pie plate

springform pan

deep-dish pie plate

tart pan

mini pie plates

How to USE THIS *Book*

FAST AND EASY ICON

Some of the recipes in this book are multistep and labor intensive. If you're looking for something that comes together without much effort, look for the Fast and Easy icon I mentioned in the introduction. Most pies do have a long bake or chill time, but the recipes marked with this icon have a quick prep time, freeing you up to do other things while your pie bakes.

GLUTEN-FREE VARIATIONS

Many fillings in this book are naturally gluten-free. The crust is where the gluten enters in. These recipes are marked with a simple fix of swapping in one of the gluten-free crusts to make the pie work for anyone who can't have gluten.

BAKE TIMES

Each pie has a bake time, normally given as a time range. Again, since ovens vary in temperature, it is best to use visual cues along with a recipe's bake time when determining whether a pie is finished. Start checking your pie at the low end of the baking time range.

PIE LABELS

Each recipe also has a pie label at the bottom of the page. This label contains the pie size for a quick reference of what dish to use. The labels also have pairing recommendations and page number references to locate pairing recipes.

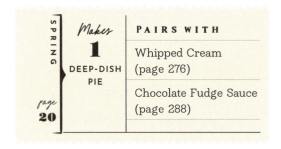

SPRING	*Makes* **1** DEEP-DISH PIE	PAIRS WITH
page **20**		Whipped Cream (page 276)
		Chocolate Fudge Sauce (page 288)

GIFTING HOMEMADE PIES

Everyone loves pie, which makes it a thoughtful, sweet, homemade gift. A 10-inch square pastry box is the perfect size for both pies and tarts. You can also box up a pie sampler for the friend who has a tough time choosing just one flavor. Small triangular boxes are also available online to package a single piece of pie. Cellophane treat bags make lovely wrappings for single pieces or mini pies. Tie up your treats with colorful ribbon and twine for a special handmade present that will be both pretty and delicious.

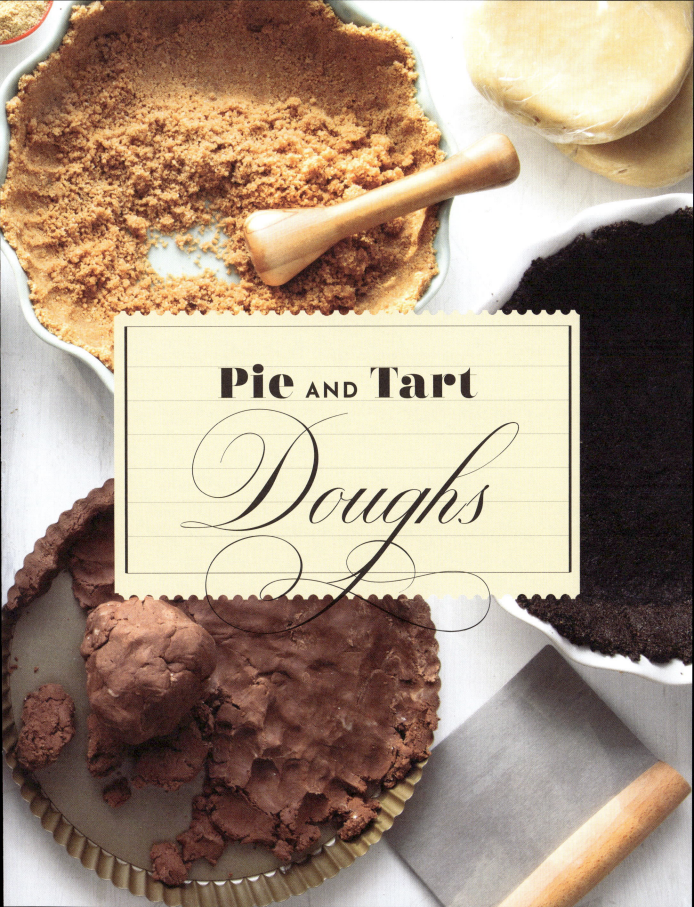

Pie AND Tart *Doughs*

Rustic
BEAUTIFUL

In Defense of an Imperfect

Crust

Many sweet and savory pies came through my childhood kitchen and were carried to dinners and gatherings. My mom loved to bake, and she had a wide repertoire of amazing treats. She also loved shortcuts. Which meant her pie crust frequently came in a red box pulled from the refrigerator. The dough she unrolled came in a perfect circle with a clean-cut edge. There were no color variations across the surface. It was a fast and tidy business to add the crust to the pie plate, saving my mom's attention for whatever rich, delicious filling she was whipping up. Now when I see a "perfect" pie crust, I think machine-made, not homemade. Making crust by hand is a messy business—butter and flour cover your hands and get under your nails, crumbs find their way to the counter and sometimes even the floor, butter flecks across the dough's surface as you roll it out, and the edge is uneven. There is nothing perfect about a handmade pie crust—but it is still beautiful.

After devoting a year to baking photo-worthy pies, I learned that crust is not meant for visual perfection. Even when you can manage to get your crust looking just as you like it, baking it will often "ruin" some part of your creation. A tender, flaky crust will not always hold its form, but it will taste amazing. So don't sweat the details or the mess or aim for visual perfection when baking your pies. Take time, slow down, and enjoy the process of forming something with your hands. We can all make pretty pies, not perfect pies; embrace the handcrafted nature of the pie, the joy of creating, the rustic beauty. Those you share a slice with will see the care and love you put into it, and they'll taste it too.

3 Methods FOR MAKING Pie Dough FOR CRUSTS

Making homemade pie dough might seem intimidating the first few times you make it, but it is much easier than you might think. The following pages contain three methods for making pie dough, which you can apply to any of the following recipes.

The key to a delicious flaky crust is keeping the fat (usually butter) cold throughout the process and cutting the butter into chunks rather than creaming it in at room temperature as you do when making a cake or cookies. The size of your butter chunks will impact how flaky the finished crust will be. When cold butter hits a hot oven, it creates steam pockets, which in turn create layers of deliciously flaky crust. So, the more chunks of butter, the more flaky pastry layers. For the flakiest crust, the butter chunks should be about the size of an almond. For a more standard crust that will be less flaky but still tender, butter chunks should be about the size of a pea. For a crust that holds its shape better and is perfect for making cutouts and crust decorations, the butter chunks should be more like a coarse crumb. These smaller pieces of butter are easiest to achieve with the food processor method.

For all three methods, be careful not to add too much water. Because different types of flour absorb liquid differently, the amount of water needed is not always the same. When the dough forms, it should not be overly sticky. If the dough is sticky, you can add more flour a tablespoon at a time. Turn the dough out onto a pastry board or counter. Divide it into the correct portions depending on the recipe and form disks. Use a bench scraper to scrape off any dough that sticks to the work surface.

Wrap each dough disk with plastic wrap and refrigerate for at least an hour before rolling it out. Dough will stay good in the refrigerator for up to two days. If you want to save it for a longer period, freeze it by placing the wrapped dough inside a resealable freezer bag and freezing for up to three months.

1 TRADITIONAL HAND METHOD

The traditional hand method is the easiest way to have full control over the size of your butter chunks. Be careful not to overwork the dough. Warm hands can melt butter. If at any stage your butter seems to be getting overly soft, stop and place the bowl in the refrigerator for fifteen minutes before continuing.

In a medium bowl, mix the dry ingredients. Slice the butter stick in half lengthwise and then into half-inch pats. Toss the butter into the flour-salt mixture with your hands to coat with flour. Flatten each piece of butter between your fingers, tossing in the flour to recoat the butter. You should still have large, flat pieces of butter ranging from the size of an almond to the size of a pea.

Sprinkle ice water over the crumb mixture. Toss to combine. Squeeze the crumbs together until a dough forms. If the dough doesn't come together, add more ice water a tablespoon at a time until you get the dough to form.

STAND MIXER WITH PASTRY ATTACHMENT METHOD

The stand mixer method is by far my favorite for making pie dough. It does require a special attachment that is not standard with most mixers. Do not attempt it with the paddle attachment, which is designed to blend ingredients. The shape of the pastry attachment is designed to cut in the butter as large and medium chunks, so you can still achieve a flaky crust. Keeping your hands out of the dough is ideal for keeping the ingredients cool and is faster and tidier than mixing by hand.

In the bowl of a stand mixer fitted with the pastry attachment, mix the dry ingredients. Slice the butter stick in half lengthwise and then into half-inch pats. Toss the butter into the flour-salt mixture and mix on low until the butter is fully coated in flour, has been cut to a smaller size, and is evenly distributed in the flour, about two minutes. You should still have medium pieces of butter ranging from the size of an almond to the size of a pea.

With the mixer running, add ice water a tablespoon at a time, watching for the dough to start to come together. When you start to see the dough forming some clumps and the mixer starts to strain a little, turn off the mixer.

FOOD PROCESSOR METHOD

Using a food processor is a fast and tidy method for making pie dough, but the machine is so efficient that you will most likely end up with butter pieces the size of coarse crumbs rather than the larger size of the other methods. This will form a crust that is less flaky but also one that holds its form better. It is a great method for dough destined for cutouts and decorative top crusts such as braided borders and complex lattice tops.

In the bowl of a food processor, add the dry ingredients and pulse to combine. Slice the butter stick in half lengthwise and then into half-inch pats. Toss the butter into the flour-salt mixture, pulse several times, and then check the size of the butter. The butter should be cut to about the size of a pea and evenly distributed in the flour.

Sprinkle the amount of water listed in the recipe over the flour mixture. Pulse three to four times to combine. You will probably need more water, which you can add outside of the food processor for better accuracy. Turn the dough out onto a pastry board or counter. If the dough is still crumbly and not holding together, sprinkle more water over the dough a tablespoon at a time and mix gently with your hands until the dough comes together.

Butter Pie Dough

This is a versatile recipe great for sweet and savory pies and galettes. I like to make this in larger batches and freeze it to use when I need it. Since this dough is used so frequently in this book, I have scaled the recipe so you can make what you need. Each pie recipe tells you the amount of dough you will need. But you can also scale up your dough if you want to create dough cutouts to ornament a pie.

To make the dough, use one of the methods listed on pages 29–31.

❋ *I like to add 1 to 2 tablespoons of buttermilk to my ice water when making this dough. It is not an essential step, and it does not need to be a precise measurement. The acid in the buttermilk prevents oxidation in the dough and will make a more tender crust. (You can also add 1 teaspoon of vodka or white vinegar if you don't have buttermilk handy.)*

SINGLE BUTTER PIE DOUGH

1¼ cups (163 g) all-purpose flour, plus more for rolling out

½ teaspoon fine sea salt

½ cup (113 g) unsalted butter

2 tablespoons ice water, plus more if needed

1½ BUTTER PIE DOUGH

1¾ cups plus 2 tablespoons (245 g) all-purpose flour, plus more for rolling out

¾ teaspoon fine sea salt

¾ cup (170 g) unsalted butter

3 tablespoons ice water, plus more if needed

DOUBLE BUTTER PIE DOUGH

2½ cups (325 g) all-purpose flour, plus more for rolling out

1 teaspoon fine sea salt

1 cup (225 g) unsalted butter

4 tablespoons ice water, plus more if needed

EXTRA-LARGE BUTTER PIE DOUGH

3¼ cups (423 g) all-purpose flour, plus more for rolling out

1½ teaspoons fine sea salt

1¼ cup (281 g) unsalted butter

5 tablespoons ice water, plus more if needed

QUADRUPLE FREEZER BUTTER PIE DOUGH

5 cups (650 g) all-purpose flour, plus more for rolling out

2 teaspoons fine sea salt

2 cups (450 g) unsalted butter

8 tablespoons ice water, plus more if needed

Maple Pie Dough

I love this recipe for a slightly sweet crust. The syrup makes the dough a little more pliable and easier to work with than traditional dough. The maple flavor is very subtle, and you can use this crust with any sweet pie.

To make the dough, use one of the methods listed on pages 29-31.
Add the maple syrup at the same time as the water.

SINGLE MAPLE PIE DOUGH

1¼ cups (163 g) all-purpose flour, plus more for rolling out

½ teaspoon fine sea salt

½ cup (113 g) unsalted butter

2 tablespoons maple syrup

1 tablespoon ice water, plus more if needed

DOUBLE MAPLE PIE DOUGH

2½ cups (325 g) all-purpose flour, plus more for rolling out

1 teaspoon fine sea salt

1 cup (225 g) unsalted butter

¼ cup maple syrup

2 tablespoons ice water, plus more if needed

Chocolate Pie Dough

A delicious variation on Butter Pie Dough, this chocolate dough pairs nicely with many of the pies in this book. I especially love making it with black cocoa, which gives it a rich Oreo-like flavor.

To make the dough, use one of the methods listed on pages 29–31.
Add the egg yolks at the same time as the water.

SINGLE CHOCOLATE PIE DOUGH

1 cup (130 g) all-purpose flour, plus more for rolling out

3 tablespoons unsweetened cocoa or black cocoa powder

3 tablespoons sugar

½ teaspoon fine sea salt

½ cup (113 g) unsalted butter

1 egg yolk

2 tablespoons ice water, plus more if needed

DOUBLE CHOCOLATE PIE DOUGH

2 cups (260 g) all-purpose flour, plus more for rolling out

⅓ cup (30 g) unsweetened cocoa or black cocoa powder

⅓ cup (66 g) sugar

1 teaspoon fine sea salt

1 cup (226 g) unsalted butter

2 egg yolks

¼ cup ice water, plus more if needed

FREEZING PIE DOUGH

Making pie dough can get a little messy, so I like to make it in large batches and freeze it. When making dough for the freezer, wrap individual disks in plastic wrap, and use masking tape and a permanent marker to write which version of dough you've made and the date it was made. Place the wrapped, labeled disks into a resealable freezer bag and freeze for up to 3 months. To use frozen pie dough, move the number of disks needed to the refrigerator at least 4 hours before using (or the day before). Remove from the refrigerator 10 minutes before rolling out.

Vegan Pie Dough

Shortening makes a great pie crust and has been a popular way to make a crust dairy-free. This recipe uses half vegetable shortening for structure and flaky results and half vegan stick butter to boost the flavor.

To make the dough, use one of the methods listed on pages 29–31.

SINGLE VEGAN PIE DOUGH

1¼ cups (163 g) all-purpose flour, plus more for rolling out

½ teaspoon fine sea salt

¼ cup (48 g) cold vegetable shortening

¼ cup (54 g) unsalted vegan butter

2 tablespoons ice water, plus more if needed

DOUBLE VEGAN PIE DOUGH

2½ cups (325 g) all-purpose flour, plus more for rolling out

1 teaspoon fine sea salt

½ cup (95 g) cold vegetable shortening

½ cup (108 g) unsalted vegan butter

¼ cup ice water, plus more if needed

Gluten-Free Pie Dough

Makes A DOUBLE CRUST

Everyone loves pie, but when someone can't eat gluten it can be disappointing to feel they need to skip dessert. That's a great time to break out this recipe. Many of the recipes in this book are gluten-free other than the crust, and can be made gluten-free simply by using this pie dough.

To make the dough, use one of the methods listed on pages 29-31. Add the egg at the same time as the water. Without the gluten, this will not be as strong as other doughs. If you have trouble rolling it out, try rolling it out on top of plastic wrap and then flipping the crust upside down into the pie plate. The plastic wrap will help keep the dough from tearing while transferring it to the baking dish. Once in place, peel the plastic wrap from the dough.

3 cups (444 g) 1-for-1 gluten-free flour, plus more for rolling out

1 teaspoon fine sea salt

1 cup (225 g) unsalted butter

1 egg, cold

6 tablespoons ice water, plus more if needed

Rolling OUT Pie Dough

To roll out dough for pie crust, remove a disk of dough from the refrigerator and allow it to sit at room temperature for 10 minutes.

Place the dough on a lightly floured surface, sprinkle some flour on top of the dough, and lightly flour the rolling pin. Press the rolling pin into the dough to see if it is soft enough to roll out. If it is still too firm, allow it to sit for a few more minutes. Roll from the center away from you. Rotate the dough a quarter turn and repeat several times, then flip the dough over and repeat. Use a bench scraper to free the dough if it sticks, then add a little more flour. Continue this process until the dough reaches the desired size.

Use a dry pastry brush to brush off any extra flour. Loosely wrap the dough around the rolling pin and use it to transfer the crust to the pie plate. Try not to stretch the dough when placing it in the dish. Trim off any extra crust with scissors, leaving about a ¾-inch overhang. For a single-crust pie, fold the extra crust under and crimp the edge. For a double-crust pie, leave the extra crust to use when connecting the top crust to the bottom.

Store the crust in the refrigerator while making the filling.

parbaked

blind-baked

PARBAKING TART CRUSTS

When parbaking or blind-baking a tart crust, do not use pie weights. Because tart crust is much thicker than pie crust, the extra weight isn't necessary, and the crust tends to stick to the parchment. Instead, simply dock the tart crust with a fork and bake per the recipe instructions.

Parbaking AND Blind-Baking *Crust*

Parbaking, or partially baking a crust, is necessary when a pie won't be in the oven long enough to fully bake the bottom of the crust. Without parbaking, the bottom crust in the finished pie might be too soft and doughy. Parbaking gives the crust a head start and will result in a sturdy, fully baked crust. Blind-baking is similar, except it completely pre-bakes the crust and is necessary when a pie's filling doesn't require any baking—such as a cold-set icebox pie. The finished pie crust should be golden brown across the whole surface and will look completely dry.

To Parbake a Crust

Preheat oven to 425°F. Roll out pie dough and place in a pie plate. Be careful not to stretch the dough when fitting it into the pie plate. Cut off any extra crust and crimp edges. Fold crimp onto the rim of the pie plate so it has something to hold on to. Use the tines of a fork to dock the crust on its bottom and sides. Refrigerate for 30 minutes. Line the crust with parchment paper and fill with pie weights or dry beans all the way to the top. Bake for 17 minutes. Remove the parchment and pie weights and dock the crust again. Bake for an additional 2 to 3 minutes or until the inside of the crust is still pale but not shiny. Allow the crust to cool completely before adding the pie filling.

To Blind-Bake a Crust

Preheat oven to 425°F. Roll out pie dough and place in a pie plate. Be careful not to stretch the dough when fitting it into the dish. Cut off any extra crust and crimp edges. Fold crimp onto the rim of the pie plate so it has something to hold on to. Use a fork to dock the crust a few times on its bottom and sides. Refrigerate for 30 minutes. Line the crust with parchment paper and fill with pie weights or dry beans all the way to the top of the crust. Bake for 17 minutes. Remove the parchment and pie weights and dock the crust again. If desired, brush the crust with Egg Wash. This will yield a more golden crust and will also form a thin barrier that will keep the crust more crisp once the filling has been added. Bake for an additional 9 to 12 minutes or until the crust is light golden across the whole surface and looks dry. Allow the crust to cool completely before adding the pie filling.

How to MAKE A *Lattice* Crust

Crust *Design*

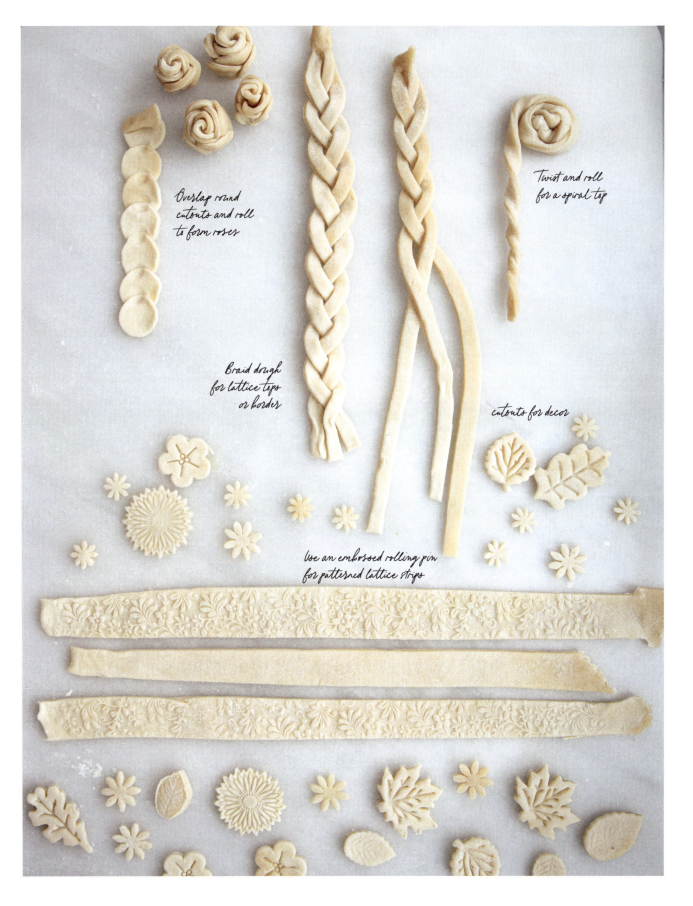

Overlap round cutouts and roll to form roses

Twist and roll for a spiral top

Braid dough for lattice tops or border

cutouts for decor

Use an embossed rolling pin for patterned lattice strips

WHAT IS A SLAB PIE?

Easier and larger than a classic pie, these rectangular desserts are to pies what bars are to cookies. They bake on a rimmed half-sheet baking pan. Because the crust is so large, it is easiest to roll the crust out in two halves and press the seam together in the pan. Crimp the edges as you would a normal pie. Slab pies are a perfect choice for a party or large gathering because they feed a crowd and are easy to cut and serve. You can find summer fruit slab pie recipes on pages 124 and 144.

Press-In Shortbread Tart Dough

Makes **1** 10-INCH TART CRUST

I've tested a lot of tart crusts over the years, and many of them are so hard, it's difficult to break off a bite with a fork. This buttery and delicious shortbread crust is delicate enough to easily break apart but strong enough to hold the tart together. Using cake flour is key to getting a nice, cookie-like crumb. This dough is not tough enough to roll out. Press the dough directly into the pan for an easy to pull together, delicious tart base.

In the bowl of a stand mixer fitted with the paddle attachment, mix butter, salt, vanilla extract, and confectioners' sugar on medium speed until light and fluffy, about 5 minutes. Add flour and mix just until combined. Press dough directly into a 10-inch tart pan, starting with the sides and finishing with the bottom. Bake the crust according to the tart recipe's instructions.

¾ cup (169 g) unsalted butter, softened

½ teaspoon fine sea salt

2 teaspoons vanilla extract

⅔ cup (73 g) confectioners' sugar

2 cups (230 g) cake flour

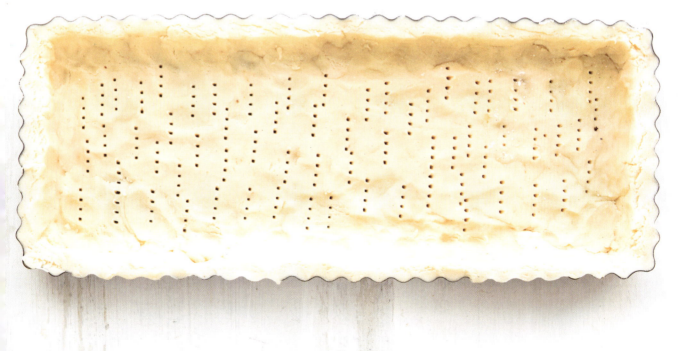

Press-In Chocolate Tart Dough

Makes **1** 10-INCH TART CRUST

This crust can be swapped in for any tart that will pair nicely with a chocolate crust. It is especially delicious with raspberry, chocolate, or caramel filling.

¾ cup (169 g) unsalted butter, softened

½ teaspoon fine sea salt

2 teaspoons vanilla extract

1 cup (110 g) confectioners' sugar

¼ cup (23 g) Dutch process cocoa

1¾ cups + 2 tablespoons (216 g) cake flour

In the bowl of a stand mixer fitted with the paddle attachment, mix butter, salt, vanilla extract, and confectioners' sugar on medium speed until light and fluffy, about 5 minutes. In a small bowl, whisk together cocoa and flour. Add to the butter mixture and mix just until combined. Press dough directly into a 10-inch tart pan, starting with the sides and finishing with the bottom. Bake the crust according to the tart recipe's instructions.

Gluten-Free Press-In Tart Dough

Makes **1** 10-INCH TART CRUST

Similar to the Shortbread Tart Crust, this crust has a nice crumb and is not too hard. Many tart recipes in this book can become gluten-free by changing to this easy press-in crust.

In the bowl of a stand mixer fitted with the paddle attachment, mix butter, salt, vanilla extract, and confectioners' sugar on medium speed until light and fluffy, about 5 minutes. Add egg and beat until fully incorporated. Add oat flour and mix just until combined. Press dough directly into a 10-inch tart pan, starting with the sides and finishing with the bottom. If the dough is too sticky to press into place, cover with plastic wrap and refrigerate for 15 minutes. Bake the crust according to the tart recipe's instructions.

½ cup (169 g) unsalted butter, softened

½ teaspoon fine sea salt

2 teaspoons vanilla extract

⅔ cup (73 g) confectioners' sugar

1 egg, room temperature

2 cups (180 g) gluten-free oat flour

TART PANS

A 10-inch round tart pan can be interchanged with 14 x 4½-inch rectangular tart pan without making any adjustments to the recipe. They have almost equal volume. Tart recipes in this book include instructions to use a 10-inch round tart pan, but you can switch to a rectangular pan for shape variation.

Crumb Crusts

Crumb crusts are so delicious and so versatile, plus they are super fast and easy to pull together. There are so many things that can be turned into crumb crusts for a variety of flavors. I've made these recipes large enough to easily cover the sides and bottom of a pie plate, so there will be no struggle to get the crust pressed in.

DEEP-DISH PIE PLATE	CLASSIC 9-INCH PIE PLATE OR 10-INCH TART PAN
2¼ cups (259 g) graham cracker crumbs ¼ cup (50 g) sugar ¼ teaspoon fine sea salt ½ cup (113 g) unsalted butter, melted	1¾ cups + 2 tablespoons (215 g) graham cracker crumbs 3 tablespoons sugar ¼ teaspoon fine sea salt 6 tablespoons (84 g) unsalted butter, melted
2¼ cups (259 g) Vanilla Wafer (page 282) or speculoos crumbs ¼ teaspoon fine sea salt ½ cup (113 g) unsalted butter, melted	1¾ cups + 2 tablespoons (215 g) Vanilla Wafer (page 282) or speculoos crumbs ¼ teaspoon fine sea salt 6 tablespoons (84 g) unsalted butter, melted
2¼ cups (259 g) Chocolate Wafer (page 280) crumbs ¼ teaspoon fine sea salt ½ cup (113 g) unsalted butter, melted	1¾ cups + 2 tablespoons (215 g) Chocolate Wafer (page 280) crumbs ¼ teaspoon fine sea salt 6 tablespoons (84 g) unsalted butter, melted
2¼ cups (259 g) Oatmeal Cookie Crisps (page 283) crumbs ¼ teaspoon fine sea salt 7 tablespoons (98 g) unsalted butter, melted	1¾ cups + 2 tablespoons (215 g) Oatmeal Cookie Crisps (page 283) crumbs ¼ teaspoon fine sea salt 5 tablespoons (70 g) unsalted butter, melted
2¼ cups (210 g) pretzel crumbs ¼ cup (50 g) sugar ½ cup (113 g) unsalted butter, melted	1¾ cups + 2 tablespoons (174 g) pretzel crumbs 3 tablespoons sugar 6 tablespoons (84 g) unsalted butter, melted

The easiest way to measure crackers or cookies before turning them into crumbs is to weigh them. Pulse crackers or cookies in a food processor until a fine crumb forms. If you don't have a food processor, you can place crackers or cookies in a gallon-sized resealable bag and crush them with a rolling pin. Combine all the dry ingredients in a medium bowl. Melt butter and pour over the crumb mixture; toss to combine. Add to pie plate or tart pan. Start by pressing the crumb up the sides of the pan and then press the remaining crumbs into the bottom. Bake according to the recipe's instructions.

All of the homemade wafer and cookie options in this book freeze nicely. I like to keep them at the ready in my freezer. However, if you don't have time to make your own, you can always use a storebought variety.

Spring

Lemon Meringue Tart

I love this twist on lemon meringue pie in tart form. For me, the proportion of crust to lemon is perfect, and it's even better with Swiss meringue instead of French meringue, which is a traditional pairing with lemon. Swiss meringue is cooked on the stove and doesn't need to go in the oven. It is softer and creamier, adding a beautiful airy sweetness to counter the tart lemon curd. This bright tart comes out looking lovely and tastes even better.

To make the crust: Preheat oven to 350°F. Press tart dough into a 10-inch tart pan. Generously dock with a fork and bake for 25 to 30 minutes or until lightly browned. While still hot, use a tamper or the back of a spoon to lightly press down the center of the crust, leaving a ¾-inch edge.

To make the lemon curd: Whisk together egg yolks, lemon zest, lemon juice, and sugar in a saucepan. Cook over medium-high heat, stirring constantly, until mixture becomes thick and coats the back of the spoon, about 8 to 10 minutes. Use an instant read thermometer to check the temperature; it should reach 170°F. Transfer to the bowl of a stand mixer fitted with the paddle attachment. Mix on low. Add butter 1 teaspoon at a time, mixing until fully combined before adding the next teaspoon of butter. Strain through a sieve into a medium bowl. Pour while still warm into the tart shell. Cover with plastic wrap and refrigerate for 2 to 3 hours.

To make the Swiss meringue: Whisk together egg whites and sugar in the top pan of a double boiler until completely incorporated (see note below). Cook, whisking continuously, for about 5 to 6 minutes or until mixture reaches 170°F. Pour into the bowl of a stand mixer fitted with the whisk attachment. Add cream of tartar. Beat on high for about 2 minutes. Add vanilla extract and continue to beat on high until stiff peaks form. Scoop or pipe onto lemon curd. Toast meringue with a kitchen torch or under the oven broiler. Keep a close watch on meringue while toasting to avoid burning. Remove sides of tart pan and serve.

Press-In Shortbread Tart Dough (page 49)

LEMON CURD
8 egg yolks

zest of 2 lemons

⅔ cup fresh lemon juice

1 cup (200g) sugar

10 tablespoons (141 g) salted butter

SWISS MERINGUE
5 egg whites

1¼ cups (250 g) sugar

½ teaspoon cream of tartar

1 teaspoon vanilla bean paste

Double boilers are sold as a set. However, if you don't have a set, you can use a small saucepan set over a larger saucepan. Fill the bottom pan with just enough water to steam-heat the top pan. The water should not touch the top pan. Personally, I use the metal bowl from my stand mixer as the top pan of the double boiler when cooking Swiss meringue. It makes for a super easy transfer from cooking to whipping.

Black Bottom Banoffee Pie

Banoffee comes from combining banana with toffee. This surprisingly easy pie creates a lovely flavor combination. It's a rich British pie with a chocolate ganache bottom, layers of dulce de leche, toffee, bananas, and whipped cream. The slightly messy deliciousness will be a hit at any gathering.

Deep-Dish Graham Cracker Crumb Crust (page 52)

EASY DULCE DE LECHE
1 (14 ounce) can sweetened condensed milk

GANACHE
4 ounces (113 g) dark chocolate, chopped

¼ cup heavy cream

TO ASSEMBLE
3 med. bananas, sliced

½ cup (78 g) toffee bits or Toffee Pecans (page 290)

Whipped Cream (page 276)

To make the dulce de leche: Remove label from the sweetened condensed milk can. Place the unopened can in a deep pot. Fill pot with water until it is 2 to 3 inches higher than the can. Place the pot on the stove over medium-high heat. Bring water to a boil, then reduce temperature so water remains at a simmer. Continue to cook for 3½ more hours. Make sure the can stays completely submerged in water, adding more as needed. After 3½ hours, remove can from water with tongs and set in the sink or on a hot pad. Allow it to cool completely before opening, about 30 minutes. Store in the refrigerator until ready to use. When you open the can, the milk should be a rich golden brown.

To make the crust: Preheat oven to 350°F. Press crumb crust into a deep-dish pie plate and bake for 6 minutes. If the crust slips down the sides of the pan while baking, use a tamper or the back of a spoon to press the crust back up the sides of the pan. Allow to cool completely.

To make the ganache: Place chopped chocolate in a heatproof bowl. Heat the heavy cream in a small saucepan over medium-high heat until steaming but not boiling. Remove from heat. Pour over chocolate and allow to sit for about 1 minute. Using a rubber spatula, stir until chocolate is melted and fully incorporated. Pour into pie crust and spread evenly across the bottom.

To assemble the pie: Slice bananas and layer on top of ganache. Spread dulce de leche over the bananas. Top with toffee bits or Toffee Pecans. Pile Whipped Cream across the top of the pie and spread to the edges. Garnish with Chocolate Curls or additional banana slices. Serve immediately or refrigerate until ready to serve.

SPRING

Makes
1
DEEP-DISH PIE

PAIRS WITH

Toffee Pecans (page 290)

Chocolate Curls (page 293)

Hummingbird Pie

Hummingbird cake originated in Jamaica and is said to have gotten its name because it's sweet enough to attract hummingbirds. This pie version of the famous Caribbean cake contains all the sweet tropical goodness baked up in a rich buttery crust.

Preheat oven to 375°F. Roll out dough on a lightly floured surface to roughly a 15-inch round. Wrap loosely around the rolling pin and transfer to a deep-dish pie plate. Cut off any extra crust and crimp edges.

To make the filling: In a small bowl, combine brown sugar, cinnamon, nutmeg, salt, and cornstarch and set aside. In a medium bowl, combine pineapple, banana, and coconut. On a cutting board, cut vanilla bean lengthwise with a sharp knife. Scrape the seeds from the vanilla bean with the edge of the knife and add to the pineapple mixture. Stir fruit until vanilla bean seeds are distributed. Add the sugar mixture to the fruit and stir until all the fruit is coated. Pour fruit mixture into the prepared crust.

To make the crumb: In a medium bowl, combine all the crumb ingredients except butter. Melt butter in a small heatproof bowl. Pour over the dry ingredients and stir with a rubber spatula. When the crumb starts to form, work with your hands until all of the ingredients are incorporated. Crumble crumb mixture evenly over fruit.

Bake for 40 to 50 minutes or until the crust and crumb are golden brown. Serve warm with Vanilla Bean Ice Cream.

Single Butter Pie Dough (page 33)

FILLING

½ cup (90 g) light brown sugar

1 teaspoon cinnamon

¼ teaspoon nutmeg

½ teaspoon fine sea salt

2 tablespoons cornstarch

4 cups (600 g) coarsely chopped pineapple, drained

1 med. banana, cut into small pieces

½ cup (50 g) sweetened flake coconut

1 vanilla bean (or 1 tablespoon vanilla bean paste)

COCONUT PECAN CRUMB

1¼ cups (163 g) all-purpose flour

¼ teaspoon fine sea salt

1 teaspoon cinnamon

½ cup (90 g) brown sugar

½ cup (53 g) chopped pecans

1 cup (100 g) sweetened flake coconut

½ cup (113 g) unsalted butter

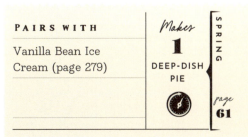

PAIRS WITH

Vanilla Bean Ice Cream (page 279)

Makes
1
DEEP-DISH PIE

SPRING

page **61**

Caramel Coconut Cream Pie

Coconut cream pies have existed for many generations and have long been a favorite of my mom's. This recipe changes up this much-loved pie and makes it even more tempting with a layer of Salted Caramel at the bottom—and even prettier with drizzled Salted Caramel over the top layer of Whipped Cream.

TOASTED COCONUT

½ cup (50 g) sweetened flake coconut

½ cup (50 g) large flake unsweetened coconut

Deep-Dish Graham Cracker or Oatmeal Cookie Crumb Crust (page 52)

COCONUT CUSTARD

4 egg yolks

⅔ cup (132 g) sugar, divided

¼ cup (40 g) cornstarch

1 vanilla bean

1 (14 ounce) can full-fat coconut cream

¾ cup heavy cream

¼ teaspoon fine sea salt

3 tablespoons unsalted butter, softened

½ cup (50 g) sweetened flake coconut

½ teaspoon coconut extract, optional

½ cup Salted Caramel, divided (page 289)

Whipped Cream (page 276)

To toast the coconut: Preheat oven to 350°F. Spread coconut on a baking sheet in a single layer, but keep the two varieties separated. Bake for 8 to 10 minutes, stirring every 3 minutes. When the coconut turns golden brown, remove from the oven and let it cool on the baking sheet.

To make the crust: Follow the recipe for the Deep-Dish Graham Cracker Crumb or the Oatmeal Cookie Crumb Crust. Add the sweetened toasted coconut to the food processor while creating the crumb. Reserve the remaining large flake coconut to garnish the finished pie. Preheat oven to 350°F. Press crumb crust into a deep-dish pie plate and bake for 6 minutes. Allow to cool completely.

To make the coconut custard: In the bowl of a stand mixer fitted with the whisk attachment, mix egg yolks, ⅓ cup sugar, and cornstarch on low. On a cutting board, cut open the vanilla bean lengthwise with a sharp knife. Scrape out the seeds with the edge of the knife and add to the yolk mixture.

In a medium saucepan, add coconut cream, heavy cream, salt, and the remaining ⅓ cup sugar. Whisk together and cook over medium heat until the mixture reaches a simmer. With the mixer still running, carefully pour the hot cream mixture into the egg yolk mixture. Mix until fully combined. Pour the mixture back into the saucepan and cook over medium-high heat, whisking constantly, until the mixture thickens and reaches 170°F, about 2 to 3 minutes.

Place a fine mesh sieve over the bowl of your stand mixer. Pour the custard through the sieve. Use a rubber spatula to get as much of the custard through as possible. Place the bowl on the mixer and mix on low with the paddle attachment. Add butter 1 teaspoon at a time, waiting until each addition is fully incorporated before adding the next. Add the coconut and the coconut extract, if using. Continue to run the mixer on low for 6 to 7 minutes to allow the custard to cool. Running the mixer prevents a skin from forming on the custard while cooling.

PAIRS WITH

Whipped Cream (page 276)

Salted Caramel (page 289)

Spread about ¼ cup of the Salted Caramel on the bottom of the prepared crust. Add the coconut custard on top of Salted Caramel. Cover with plastic wrap pressed directly onto the surface of the custard. Refrigerate for at least 2 hours or overnight. When ready to serve, remove the plastic wrap and cover the top with fresh Whipped Cream, reserved toasted coconut, and drizzles of remaining Salted Caramel.

Mango Tarte Tatin

The first tartes tatin were made at the Hotel Tatin in the South of France in the late 1800s. That original version–an apple baked with a crust and then turned upside down–was said to be a mistake when one of the owners was in a hurry to make an apple pie. The resulting fruit in caramelized sugar was so beloved that this upside-down tart has endured and evolved to many variations. This mango version is a delicious and bright addition to a spring table.

To make rough puff pastry: On a lightly floured surface, roll out pie dough into a ¼-inch thick rectangle. Use a bench scraper to neaten the edges and make them as straight as you can. (They don't have to be perfect.) Fold the dough as you would a letter—fold the top third down, then the bottom third up. Rotate dough 90 degrees and roll it out to a ¼-inch-thick rectangle again. Repeat the letter fold. Wrap dough in plastic wrap and refrigerate for 30 minutes.

Remove dough from the refrigerator and repeat step 1, rolling and folding the dough two more times. Then wrap tightly in plastic wrap and refrigerate for 30 more minutes.

Preheat oven to 375°F. Generously grease a 9-inch round cake pan with butter and line the bottom with a round of parchment paper.

In a medium bowl, mix together brown sugar and salt. Pour melted butter over and stir until combined. With a sharp knife on a cutting board, cut the vanilla bean lengthwise. Scrape the seeds from the vanilla bean and add to the sugar mixture and stir until combined. Spread the sugar mixture on the bottom of the prepared pan.

Peel and slice mangos. Lay mango slices in the sugar mixture, slightly overlapping each other. On a lightly floured surface, roll out the rough puff pastry to a 10-inch round. Place over mangos and tuck in the sides inside the pan edges. Bake for 45 to 55 minutes or until the crust is golden brown. Allow to sit in the pan for 10 minutes and then invert onto a serving plate—one with sides to keep any liquid from running off the plate. Serve warm with Whipped Cream or Vanilla Bean Ice Cream.

Single Butter or Maple Pie Dough (pages 33, 34)

1 cup (180 g) brown sugar

¼ teaspoon fine sea salt

5 tablespoons (70 g) unsalted butter, melted

1 vanilla bean

2 lg. mangoes

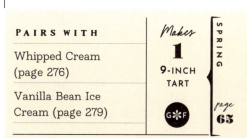

PAIRS WITH

Whipped Cream (page 276)

Vanilla Bean Ice Cream (page 279)

Makes
1
9-INCH
TART

G❋F

Salted Maple Chess Pie

A variation on the traditional Southern chess pie, this simple salty sweet pie is a perfect treat in the spring when the maple trees start to wake and sugaring begins. Use grade B or dark maple syrup for the most maple flavor.

Single Maple Pie Dough
(page 34)

½ cup (113 g) unsalted butter, melted

½ cup (90 g) light brown sugar

¾ cup maple syrup

1 tablespoon vanilla extract

3 eggs, room temperature

2 tablespoons all-purpose flour

2 tablespoons fine cornmeal

¼ teaspoon fine sea salt

TO GARNISH
1 pinch flaked sea salt

Parbake the crust in a 9-inch pie plate according to the instructions on page 41, then reduce oven temperature to 325°F.

In the bowl of a stand mixer fitted with the paddle attachment, beat butter, sugar, maple syrup, and vanilla until fully incorporated. Add eggs one at a time, mixing between each addition. In a small bowl, combine flour, cornmeal, and salt. Add to the butter mixture. Mix just until combined. Scrape the sides and bottom of the bowl to ensure even mixing. Pour into the cooled parbaked crust.

Bake for 45 to 50 minutes or until the center of the pie is only slightly jiggly. Allow the pie to cool completely before cutting. Garnish with flaked sea salt and serve with Whipped Cream.

SPRING

Makes
1
CLASSIC-
SIZED PIE

PAIRS WITH

Whipped Cream
(page 276)

Brown Butter Pie

Inspired by Milk Bar Pie, this gooey, buttery pie is utterly addictive. The Oatmeal Cookie crust forms a solid, delicious, crisp base to the rich brown butter filling. Keep your slices small because this one is intense. Pair it with a steaming cup of coffee for a sweet afternoon treat.

Set a medium heatproof bowl near the stove. Melt butter in a medium saucepan over medium-high heat. Whisk butter and continue to cook until small brown specks appear near the bottom of the pan. Butter should have turned amber and have a nutty aroma. Pour into the bowl to prevent further cooking and possibly burning the butter. Allow to cool.

Preheat oven to 350°F. Press crust into a 9-inch pie plate and set aside.

In the bowl of a stand mixer fitted with the paddle attachment, combine cooled brown butter and brown sugar. Mix on medium speed until fully combined. Add eggs, egg yolks, and vanilla extract and mix until combined. Using a rubber spatula, scrape the bottom and sides of the bowl to ensure even mixing. In a small bowl, whisk together salt and flour and add to the butter mixture. Beat just until combined. Pour into the prepared crust and bake for 30 to 40 minutes or until the top is golden brown and slightly puffed. Allow the pie to cool completely and then cover and refrigerate for at least 2 hours before cutting. Resist cutting the pie while hot. The gooey center will still be very runny until it has fully cooled. Serve cold with Vanilla Bean Ice Cream or Whipped Cream.

Classic Oatmeal Cookie Crumb Crust (page 52)

¾ cup (169 g) unsalted butter

1½ cups (270 g) brown sugar

2 eggs

2 egg yolks

1 tablespoon vanilla extract

⅔ cup (87 g) all-purpose flour

½ teaspoon fine sea salt

PAIRS WITH

Vanilla Bean Ice Cream (page 279)

Whipped Cream (page 276)

Makes
1
CLASSIC-SIZED PIE

SPRING

Mississippi Mud Pie

Ooey, gooey, and delicious—the rich, dark, chocolatey layers of this pie will more than cover your chocolate cravings. The origin of this pie and its exact recipe are debated, but the muddy banks of the Mississippi were surely an inspiration for this slightly messy but satisfying pie.

Deep-Dish Chocolate Wafer Crumb Crust (page 52)

BROWNIE BOTTOM

½ cup (113 g) salted butter, melted

½ cup (90 g) brown sugar

½ cup (100 g) sugar

2 teaspoons vanilla extract

2 eggs, room temperature

½ cup (65 g) all-purpose flour

½ cup (45 g) unsweetened cocoa powder

⅓ cup Chocolate Fudge Sauce (page 288), plus more for serving

CHOCOLATE CREAM

5 ounces (142 g) dark chocolate

1 cup half and half, divided

2 tablespoons cornstarch

3 egg yolks

¾ cup (150 g) sugar

¼ cup (56 g) salted butter, room temperature

2 tablespoons unsweetened cocoa powder

⅓ cup (36 g) confectioners' sugar

2 teaspoons vanilla extract

To make the brownie bottom: Preheat oven to 350°F. Press crust into a deep-dish pie plate. In a medium mixing bowl, combine melted butter, sugars, eggs, and vanilla with a rubber spatula. In a small bowl, whisk together flour and cocoa. Add the flour mixture to the butter mixture and fold together just until combined. Pour batter into the unbaked crust. Bake 20 to 25 minutes or until a cake tester inserted into the edge of the brownies comes out clean but they are still jiggly in the center. Allow to cool. Spread Chocolate Fudge Sauce over the cooled brownie bottom.

To make the chocolate cream: Chop chocolate into small pieces and place in a heatproof bowl. Place a fine mesh sieve over the bowl and set aside. Mix about 2 tablespoons of the half and half with the cornstarch in a small bowl to make a slurry. In a medium saucepan, whisk together egg yolks, sugar, and the remainder of the half and half. Add the slurry and whisk to combine. Cook over medium-high heat, stirring constantly, until mixture becomes thick and coats the back of the spoon, 8 to 10 minutes. Use an instant read thermometer to check the temperature; it should reach 170°F. Pour hot mixture into the sieve, using a rubber spatula to help press it through, directly onto the chopped chocolate. Allow hot mixture to sit on chocolate for about 1 minute, then stir until the chocolate has melted and is completely incorporated. Allow the mixture to cool completely.

In the bowl of a stand mixer fitted with the whisk attachment, beat butter, cocoa, confectioners' sugar, vanilla extract, and salt on high until light and fluffy, about 5 minutes. Add the cooled chocolate mixture and beat on high for 5 additional minutes, stopping once to scrape down the sides and bottom of the bowl to ensure even mixing. Spread over brownie bottom. Cover with plastic wrap and refrigerate for at least 4 hours or overnight.

Before serving, drizzle a thin layer of additional Chocolate Fudge Sauce over the chocolate cream. Top with Whipped Cream and Chocolate Curls. Serve immediately.

SPRING

Makes

1

DEEP-DISH PIE

PAIRS WITH
Whipped Cream (page 276)
Chocolate Curls (page 293)

Birthday Sugar Cookie Confetti Pie

With flavors akin to a layered vanilla birthday cake with a hint of almond extract, this is the pie you can add candles to and gather around to sing "Happy Birthday." It has a sugar cookie base and a creamy, confetti filling with a buttercream garnish–an ultra-sweet treat that is truly a celebration in pie form.

Preheat oven to 325°F. Press crust into a deep-dish pie plate. Line a baking sheet with parchment paper or a silicone baking mat and set aside.

To make the sugar cookie: In the bowl of a stand mixer fitted with the paddle attachment, beat butter and sugar on medium speed until light and fluffy, about 5 minutes. Add egg and extracts and mix until combined. In a small bowl, combine flour, salt, baking powder, and sprinkles. Add to the butter mixture and beat until combined. Press ⅔ of the dough into the pie plate, on top of the crumb crust. Bake for 30 to 35 minutes. Form a ball with the remaining dough and place on the prepared baking sheet, then flatten to about ¾-inch thick. Store covered in the refrigerator while the pie bakes. While the pie is cooling, uncover cookie dough and bake for 18 to 20 minutes. Allow the pie and the cookie to cool completely. Place the cookie in an airtight container.

To make the cheesecake filling: In the bowl of a stand mixer fitted with the whisk attachment, beat cream cheese on medium speed until fluffy, about 4 minutes. Add confectioners' sugar, vanilla, and heavy cream and beat on high until soft peaks form, about 5 minutes, stopping once to scrape the bottom and sides of the bowl. Spread the mixture on top of the cooled cookie pie. Cover and refrigerate for at least an hour or overnight.

(continued)

Deep-Dish Vanilla Wafer Crumb Crust (page 52)

SUGAR COOKIE

¾ cup (169 g) unsalted butter, softened

¾ cup (150 g) sugar

1 egg, room temperature

½ teaspoon almond extract

1 teaspoon vanilla extract

1¾ cups (201 g) cake flour

½ teaspoon fine sea salt

1 teaspoon baking powder

½ cup sprinkles (not nonpareil)

CHEESECAKE FILLING

8 ounces (227 g) cream cheese, softened

⅔ cup (73 g) confectioners' sugar

2 teaspoons vanilla extract

1 cup heavy cream

½ cup sprinkles (not nonpareil), plus more to garnish

BUTTERCREAM GARNISH (OPTIONAL)

½ cup (113 g) unsalted butter, softened

2½ cups (275 g) confectioners' sugar

2 tablespoons heavy cream

2 teaspoons vanilla extract

If using, make the buttercream garnish just before serving: In the bowl of a stand mixer fitted with the paddle attachment, beat butter and confectioners' sugar on medium speed until fully incorporated and light and fluffy, about 5 minutes. Add heavy cream and vanilla and beat just until combined. Transfer the buttercream to a pastry bag fitted with a large tip. Pipe onto the edge of the pie. Crumble the reserved cookie and garnish pie with cookie bits and more sprinkles.

Key Lime Tart

Key Lime Tart gets its name from the small limes that come from the Florida Keys. Key limes are a little less tart than the more common Persian limes, but you can swap in the easier-to-find limes in this recipe and it will still be a sweet-tart dreamy dessert. Top with Whipped Cream and lime slices for a cheery tart perfect for an Easter spread or even just a simple snack.

Preheat oven to 325°F. Press crust into a 10-inch tart pan and set aside.

In the bowl of a stand mixer fitted with the whisk attachment, beat sweetened condensed milk, egg yolks, salt, and lime zest on medium-high speed for 3 to 4 minutes. Add lime juice and mix on low until completely incorporated. Immediately pour into the prepared crust and bake for 17 to 20 minutes or until the filling is set at the edges and slightly jiggly in the center. Center should reach 145°F on an instant read thermometer.

Allow the tart to cool completely, cover with plastic wrap, and refrigerate for at least 2 hours. When ready to serve, top with Whipped Cream and garnish with lime zest and lime slices.

Classic Graham Cracker Crumb Crust (page 52)

FILLING

1 (14 ounce) can sweetened condensed milk

3 egg yolks

¼ teaspoon fine sea salt

2 teaspoons key lime zest, plus more to garnish

⅔ cup fresh key lime juice (from about 12 key limes)

TO GARNISH

Whipped Cream (page 276)

lime slices

PAIRS WITH

Whipped Cream (page 276)

Makes
1
10-INCH ROUND TART

SPRING

page
77

WHEN THERE'S NO TIME FOR HOMEMADE ICE CREAM

When I was growing up, my mother had a full repertoire of delicious ice cream dessert recipes. Her recipes always called for softened storebought vanilla ice cream. When I started this book, I set out to raise the bar on the concept with fresh ingredients, including from-scratch ice cream. But if you don't have the equipment or the time, you can replace the ice cream in this pie with 1 quart of storebought vanilla. Allow the ice cream to get soft enough to stir (but not fully melted), and then mix in the remaining ingredients.

Brown Butter Toffee Ice Cream Pie

Maybe spring is still too chilly for ice cream, but I would be willing to eat a slice of this frozen, salty, sweet goodness in any season. The brown butter adds depth to the vanilla ice cream, and the swirls of chocolate and chunks of toffee make it a flavor combination win, all packed in a chocolate crust.

SPECIAL EQUIPMENT
Ice Cream Maker

Classic Chocolate Wafer Crumb Crust (page 52)

½ cup (113 g) salted butter

1½ cups heavy cream

1¾ cups whole milk, divided

2 tablespoons cornstarch

⅓ cup maple syrup

½ cup (90 g) brown sugar

1 vanilla bean (or 1 tablespoon vanilla bean paste)

5 ounces (142 g) toffee bar, coarsely chopped

¼ cup Salted Caramel (page 289)

¼ cup Chocolate Fudge Sauce (page 288), plus additional to garnish

TO GARNISH
1½ ounces (43 g) toffee bar, coarsely chopped

Melt butter in a medium or large saucepan over medium-high heat. Whisk and continue to cook until small brown specks appear near the bottom of the pan. Butter should have a nutty aroma and become a golden brown. Whisk in heavy cream and 1½ cups milk.

In a small bowl, whisk remaining ¼ cup milk with cornstarch until all lumps have dissolved. Add to the saucepan. Add maple syrup and brown sugar and whisk to combine. On a cutting board, cut open the vanilla bean lengthwise with a sharp knife. Scrape out the seeds with the edge of the knife and add to the mixture. Continue cooking over medium-high heat until the mixture just about reaches a boil. Reduce heat to medium-low and continue cooking until it thickens, about 5 more minutes. Allow to cool and then cover and chill in the refrigerator for at least 2 hours or overnight.

To make the crust: Preheat oven to 350°F. Press the crumb crust into a 9-inch pie plate and bake for 6 minutes. If the crust slips down the sides of the pan while baking, use a tamper or the back of a spoon to press the crust back up the sides of the pan. Allow to cool completely.

Add the chilled cream mixture to an ice cream maker and follow the manufacturer's instructions to churn into ice cream. Near the end of churning time, add chopped toffee to the ice cream. When ice cream is finished, scoop into cooled pie crust. Swirl in ¼ cup each Salted Caramel and Chocolate Fudge Sauce. Cover and freeze for at least 2 hours or overnight. When ready to serve, garnish with more chopped toffee and Chocolate Fudge Sauce.

✽ *One of the easiest ways to cut this pie is to pop it out of the pie plate, place the pie on a cutting board, and cut with a large chef's knife. Serve cut pieces immediately or return them to pie plate, cover, and store in the freezer.*

Makes **1** CLASSIC-SIZED PIE

Whoopie Pies

Though no one knows for sure where the name for these amazing packages of chocolatey sweetness came from, one story says that when people found them in packed lunches, they would shout "Whoopie!" with joy. I remember eating and loving these on the rare occasions my mom would make them. They are part pie, part cake, and part sandwich cookie. They've also been known as black moons and BFOs (big fat Oreos). Whatever you call them, these old-time treats pack a lot of sweet satisfaction in a handheld pie.

CAKES

1 cup (225 g) unsalted butter, softened

¾ cup (150 g) sugar

¾ cup (135 g) brown sugar

2 teaspoons vanilla extract

2 eggs, room temperature

2⅔ cups (346 g) all-purpose flour

¾ cup (68 g) unsweetened cocoa powder

1 teaspoon baking powder

½ teaspoon baking soda

½ teaspoon fine sea salt

1 teaspoon espresso powder

⅔ cup buttermilk, room temperature

SWISS MERINGUE BUTTERCREAM

5 egg whites

1½ cups (300 g) sugar

¼ teaspoon fine sea salt

½ teaspoon cream of tartar

1½ cups (338 g) unsalted butter, room temperature

1 tablespoon vanilla bean paste

To make the cakes: Preheat oven to 350°F. Line a baking sheet with parchment paper or a silicone baking mat.

In the bowl of a stand mixer fitted with the paddle attachment, cream butter and sugars until light and fluffy, about 5 minutes. Add vanilla extract and eggs and mix until fully incorporated. In a medium bowl, sift together flour, unsweetened cocoa, baking powder, baking soda, salt, and espresso powder. Add about half of the flour mixture to the butter mixture and mix on low. Add about half of the buttermilk while the mixer is running. Add the remaining flour mixture, then the remaining buttermilk. Mix until combined. Scrape the bottom and sides of the bowl with a rubber spatula to ensure even mixing. Scoop dough onto the prepared baking sheet with a 1.5-ounce cookie scoop. Leave about 3 inches between each cake. They expand a lot while baking. Bake for 10 minutes. Allow cakes to rest on the pan for about 5 minutes before transferring to a cooling rack. Allow to cool completely.

To make the Swiss meringue buttercream: In the top pan of a double boiler, whisk together egg whites, sugar, and salt until completely incorporated. Cook, whisking continuously, until the mixture reaches 170°F, about 5 to 6 minutes. Pour into the bowl of a stand mixer fitted with the whisk attachment. Add cream of tartar. Beat on medium speed for about 2 minutes, then increase speed to high. Continue beating until stiff peaks form. Allow meringue to cool to room temperature before moving on to the next step.

Switch to the paddle attachment. With the mixer running on medium speed, add room temperature butter 1 tablespoon at a time. Butter should be soft but still cool. Allow each addition to fully incorporate before adding the next. Add vanilla bean paste and mix just until combined.

If Swiss meringue buttercream comes out soupy, place the bowl in the refrigerator for 10 minutes, then mix on high again. Repeat refrigerating and mixing until buttercream becomes light and fluffy after mixing.

Fill a pastry bag fitted with a large round tip with buttercream. Divide cakes into pairs, matching sizes. Pipe a thick layer of buttercream on the flat side of one cake and top with its pair. Press carefully together. Cakes are fragile and break easily. Serve immediately or store in an airtight container in the refrigerator until ready to eat.

Oatmeal Carmelita Pie

My colleague Brianna brings one of her childhood favorite treats, Carmelita Bars, into work, and they are always a big hit with everyone in the office. She shared the recipe with me so I could adapt it into a pie. With a crisp Oatmeal Cookie crust and gooey Salted Caramel filling, this new version of her classic treat is sure to be a hit.

½ cup (60 g) chopped walnuts

Preheat oven 350°F. Press crust into a deep-dish pie plate and set aside.

In a medium bowl, combine flour, oatmeal, brown sugar, baking soda, and salt and mix to combine. Pour melted butter over mixture and mix until crumbly clumps form. Place half of the crumble in the prepared pie crust. Cover with Salted Caramel, chocolate chips, and walnuts. Spread remaining oatmeal crumble evenly on top.

Place on a baking sheet to catch any drips. The pie will bubble while baking. Bake for about 40 to 45 minutes or until the top is golden brown, the edges have set, and the center is still a little jiggly. Serve warm with Caramel Shards and a drizzle of Chocolate Fudge Sauce.

Deep-Dish Oatmeal Cookie Crumb Crust (page 52)

1½ cups (195 g) all-purpose flour

1½ cups (120 g) old-fashioned oatmeal

1 cup (180 g) brown sugar

1 teaspoon baking soda

½ teaspoon fine sea salt

1 cup (225 g) unsalted butter, melted

1¼ cups Salted Caramel (page 289)

6 ounces (170 g) dark chocolate chips

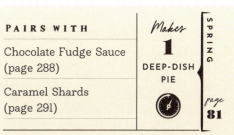

PAIRS WITH

Chocolate Fudge Sauce
(page 288)

Caramel Shards
(page 291)

Makes
1
DEEP-DISH
PIE

SPRING

page
81

Jam Hand Pies

Toaster pastries were a household treat at our house when I was growing up, but they were nothing like these handheld pies with their flaky crusts and homemade fillings. You can use your favorite jam flavor or create multiple flavors with different fruit preserves.

Double Butter Pie Dough
(page 33)

FILLING
¾ cup jam
Sweet Egg Wash (page 275)

ICING
2 ounces (57 g) cream cheese, softened

¼ cup heavy cream

1 teaspoon vanilla bean paste

1 cup (110 g) confectioners' sugar

sprinkles, to garnish

Preheat oven to 375°F and line two baking sheets with parchment paper or silicone baking mats and set aside.

On a lightly floured surface, roll out the first disk of pie dough to ⅛-inch thick. With a knife or bench scraper, cut out 4½ × 3¼-inch rectangles. Cut as many rectangles as you can, then gather the scraps and roll out dough two more times to get as many rectangles as possible. Repeat with the second disk of dough. You should have 18 rectangles total.

Place the first dough rectangle on a prepared baking sheet. Add 4 teaspoons of jam to the center of the rectangle. Spread the jam, leaving a ½-inch border. Brush Egg Wash on the border. Cover with a second dough rectangle. With the tines of a fork, crimp edges of pastry and poke a few holes in the top. Repeat with remaining dough rectangles, spacing them out over both baking sheets. Brush the tops with Egg Wash. Bake one sheet at a time, storing the second sheet in the refrigerator, for 22 to 25 minutes or until golden brown on top. Transfer to a cooling rack and allow to cool completely.

To make the icing: In the bowl of a stand mixer fitted with the whisk attachment, beat cream cheese and heavy cream on high until soft peaks form, about 3 minutes. Add vanilla and confectioners' sugar and mix just until incorporated. With an offset spatula, spread onto the tops of the cooled pastries. Top with sprinkles and serve immediately. Store leftovers in an airtight container for up to 3 days or freeze for up to 2 months.

Chocolate Silk Pie

This recipe is based on a tried-and-true recipe that my mom and her cousin Leah made often when I was growing up. Its addictive, fluffy, rich flavor made it one of my most frequent requests and a popular recipe swapped among my mom's church community. Some versions of this pie have raw eggs, but this recipe brings the eggs to a temperature that makes them safe to eat.

To make the crust: Roll out dough on a lightly floured surface to roughly a 15-inch round. Wrap loosely around the rolling pin and transfer to a deep-dish pie plate. Cut off any extra crust and crimp edges. Blind-bake the crust according to the instructions on page 41.

To make the filling: Place chopped chocolate in a heatproof bowl. Set a fine mesh sieve over the bowl and set aside. Whisk together eggs, egg yolks, and sugar in a medium saucepan. Cook over medium-high heat, stirring constantly, until mixture becomes thick and coats the back of the spoon, 8 to 10 minutes. Use an instant read thermometer to check the temperature; it should reach 170°F. Pour hot mixture into the sieve, using a rubber spatula to press the mixture through, directly onto the chocolate. Allow to sit for about 1 minute and then stir until chocolate has melted and is completely incorporated. Allow the mixture to cool completely.

In the bowl of a stand mixer fitted with the paddle attachment, beat butter, vanilla extract, and salt on high until light and fluffy, about 3 minutes. Add cooled chocolate mixture and beat on high for 5 minutes, stopping once to scrape down the sides and bottom of the bowl to ensure even mixing. Cover with plastic wrap and refrigerate for at least 1 hour.

In the bowl of a stand mixer fitted with the whisk attachment, add heavy cream and confectioners' sugar. Beat on high until stiff peaks form. Fold into cooled chocolate mixture. Pour into prepared crust. Cover and refrigerate for at least 2 hours or overnight.

Before serving, top with more Whipped Cream and Dark Chocolate Curls.

Single Butter Pie Dough (page 33)

FILLING

7 ounces (198 g) dark chocolate, chopped

4 eggs

2 egg yolks

1¼ cups (250 g) sugar

¾ cup (169 g) unsalted butter, room temperature

2 teaspoons vanilla extract

¼ teaspoon fine sea salt

1 cup heavy cream

2 tablespoons confectioners' sugar

TO GARNISH

Whipped Cream (page 276)

Dark Chocolate Curls (page 293)

PAIRS WITH

Whipped Cream
(page 276)

Dark Chocolate Curls
(page 293)

Makes

1

DEEP-DISH
PIE

G✸F

SPRING

Irish Cream Espresso Brownie Pie

When it comes to celebrating St. Patrick's Day, Irish cream with coffee is a classic pairing. This pie combines those delicious flavors with an espresso brownie base topped with an Irish coffee custard and, for good measure, a rich and creamy whipped topping.

Deep-Dish Chocolate Wafer Crumb Crust (page 52)

CUSTARD

½ cup (100 g) sugar

4 egg yolks

⅓ cup espresso or strong coffee

2 tablespoons Irish cream liqueur

¾ cup half and half

2 tablespoons cornstarch

BROWNIE BOTTOM

½ cup (113 g) unsalted butter, melted and cooled

½ cup (90 g) brown sugar

½ cup (100 g) granulated sugar

2 eggs, room temperature

2 teaspoons vanilla extract

½ cup (65 g) all-purpose flour

¼ teaspoon fine sea salt

2 teaspoons espresso powder

½ cup (46 g) unsweetened cocoa powder

To make the custard: In the bowl of a stand mixer fitted with the whisk attachment, mix egg yolks and sugar on medium speed for 2 to 3 minutes until fully combined and smooth. In a medium saucepan, combine espresso, Irish cream, half and half, and cornstarch. Cook over medium-high heat, whisking constantly, until the mixture simmers. Do not allow it to boil. Remove from heat. With the mixer running on low, carefully pour about half of the espresso mixture into the egg yolk mixture. Run the mixer until completely incorporated. Pour the mixture back into the saucepan and return to the stove. Cook over medium heat, stirring constantly, until it becomes thick and coats the back of a spoon, about 8 to 10 minutes. The temperature should reach 170°F on an instant read thermometer. Pour the mixture through a fine mesh sieve into a medium bowl. Use a rubber spatula to press it through the sieve. To cover, press plastic wrap directly to the surface of the custard. Refrigerate for at least 2 hours or overnight.

To make the brownie bottom: Press crumb crust into a deep-dish pie plate. Preheat oven to 350°F. In a medium mixing bowl, combine melted butter, sugars, eggs, and vanilla with a rubber spatula. In a small bowl, whisk together flour, salt, and espresso powder. Sift cocoa into flour mixture and whisk to combine. Add flour mixture to the butter mixture and fold together just until combined. Pour batter into the unbaked crumb crust. Bake 20 to 25 minutes or until a cake tester inserted into the edge of the brownies comes out clean. Allow to cool.

To make the topping: In the bowl of a stand mixer fitted with the whisk attachment, add cream cheese and heavy cream. Beat on medium speed for 4 to 5 minutes or until medium peaks form. Add confectioners' sugar and vanilla extract. Mix until combined. Mix about ⅓ cup chilled custard into the

PAIRS WITH

Chocolate Fudge Sauce (page 288)

Chocolate Wafer Cookies (page 280)

TOPPING

2 ounces (57 g) cold cream cheese

1 cup heavy cream

2 tablespoons confectioners' sugar

2 teaspoons vanilla extract

TO GARNISH

chocolate-covered espresso beans

Chocolate Wafer Cookies
(page 280)

Chocolate Fudge Sauce
(page 288)

whipped cream. Add the rest of the custard to the top of the cooled brownie, spreading evenly with an offset spatula. Top with the whipped cream mixture by either piping with a pastry bag fitted with a large star tip or simply by spreading the whipped cream on top. Garnish with chocolate-covered espresso beans, Chocolate Fudge Sauce, or Chocolate Wafer Cookies if desired.

Serve immediately or store in the refrigerator until ready to serve.

Grasshopper Tart

I spent a spring semester studying in Ireland with my cousin Betsy, and the thing that surprised us most about St. Patrick's Day was the volume of Americans that flooded Dublin. The holiday really seemed more important to the Americans than to the Irish. Perhaps we've altered the holiday to our own American version, but having something green here (check out the Chicago River) seems an essential component to Saint Paddy's Day in the States. This tart is a lovely green, minty treat that fits the bill. Top it with Whipped Cream to create a festive and fun dessert.

Preheat oven to 350°F. Press the crumb crust into a 10-inch tart pan and bake for 6 minutes. Allow to cool.

In a small bowl, combine cold water and gelatin. Set aside and allow it to bloom, about 5 to 10 minutes. Add chopped white chocolate to a heatproof bowl. In a medium saucepan, add heavy cream and crème de menthe syrup. Cook over medium-high heat until steaming and just about to boil. Remove from heat. Stir the bloomed gelatin into the cream mixture while it is still steaming hot. Pour the mixture over the white chocolate and let it sit for about 1 minute. With a rubber spatula, stir until chocolate is melted and fully combined. Pour into the crust, cover with plastic wrap, and refrigerate for at least 1 hour.

To make the ganache: Add chopped chocolate to a heatproof bowl. Heat heavy cream over medium-high heat until steaming but not boiling. Remove from heat. Pour cream over chocolate and allow to sit for about 1 minute. Using a rubber spatula, stir until chocolate is melted and fully incorporated. Allow ganache to sit for 5 to 10 minutes, until it thickens a little, then pour over the cooled tart. Cover and refrigerate for 1 hour or until ganache sets. Keep in the refrigerator until ready to serve.

❋ *To make this into an ornamented tart, top with Whipped Cream, chocolate sprinkles, green mint chocolate chips, and/or shamrock-shaped chocolate cookies.*

Classic Chocolate Wafer Crumb Crust (page 52) (swap in Mint Oreos with the filling for more mint flavor)

FILLING

3 tablespoons cold water

1 teaspoon unflavored gelatin

8 ounces (227 g) white chocolate, coarsely chopped

1¼ cups heavy cream

¼ cup crème de menthe syrup

GANACHE TOPPING

4 ounces (113 g) milk chocolate, chopped

½ cup heavy cream

Blooming gelatin means to hydrate the powder, making it soft and pliable with a gel-like consistency. This step is important in getting a smooth consistency in your finished pie.

PAIRS WITH

Whipped Cream
(page 276)

Makes

1

10-INCH
TART

S P R I N G

page
89

Rhubarb Raspberry Pie

As one of the first things to pop from the thawing earth in spring, rhubarb represents new chances and hope to me. My family has had a soft spot for this extraordinarily tart vegetable for generations. It's a joy when I first see it in the spring and is a reminder that the long winter is ending and the harvests of summer fruits are soon to appear. Strawberries are a traditional pairing with rhubarb, but I prefer raspberries because they are readily available any season and the flavors meld beautifully when baked with the tart rhubarb.

Double Butter Pie Dough
(page 33)

2 eggs, room temperature

1½ cups (300 g) sugar

2 tablespoons salted butter, melted

1 tablespoon vanilla bean paste

¼ cup (33 g) all-purpose flour

3 cups (317 g) chopped rhubarb

2 cups (250 g) raspberries

Egg Wash (page 275)

Preheat oven to 375°F.

Roll out one disk of dough on a lightly floured surface to roughly a 15-inch round. Wrap loosely around the rolling pin and transfer to a deep-dish pie plate. Cut off any extra crust.

In the bowl of a stand mixer fitted with the whisk attachment, beat eggs and sugar for 2 to 3 minutes. Add butter, vanilla bean paste, and flour and beat just until combined. Remove bowl from stand mixer and mix in rhubarb and raspberries by hand with a rubber spatula. Pour into prepared pie crust.

Roll out the second portion of dough and assemble the crust using your desired top crust method (see pages 42–47). Crimp top and bottom crusts together and cut a few vents in the top, then brush with Egg Wash. Bake for 50 to 60 minutes or until top crust is golden brown and filling is bubbling. Allow to cool for 20 minutes before cutting. Serve warm with Whipped Cream or Vanilla Bean Ice Cream.

SPRING

Makes
1
DEEP-DISH PIE

PAIRS WITH

Vanilla Bean Ice Cream (page 279)

Whipped Cream (page 276)

Rhubarb Crumb Tart

This absolutely delicious tart is a melding of my mom's rhubarb bars and my go-to mango crumb tart recipe. The tartness of the rhubarb balances beautifully with the buttery sweet crumb. This spring treat never lasts long at my house; it makes a lovely snack with coffee while it lasts. With its pinkish red filling peeking through the crumb, it also makes a beautiful and tasty gift.

Preheat oven to 350°F. Press tart dough into a 10-inch tart pan and set aside.

To make the filling: Add rhubarb and sugar to a medium saucepan. Mix cornstarch with water until completely dissolved. Add cornstarch slurry and vanilla to the saucepan. Cook over medium-high heat until the rhubarb has mostly broken down and the mixture thickens, about 10 to 12 minutes.

To make the crumb: In a medium bowl, combine flour, salt, cinnamon, and sugars. Pour butter over the flour mixture and stir until a crumb forms. Evenly sprinkle over the rhubarb mixture. Bake for about 40 to 45 minutes, or until the crumb and crust are golden brown.

Allow tart to cool for 15 minutes before removing from the pan. Serve warm with Vanilla Bean Ice Cream.

Press-In Shortbread Tart Dough (page 49)

FILLING

3½ cups (370 g) chopped rhubarb

1¼ cups (250 g) sugar

2 tablespoons cornstarch

¼ cup water

1 teaspoon vanilla extract

CRUMB

1¼ cups (163 g) all-purpose flour

¼ teaspoon fine sea salt

½ teaspoon cinnamon

½ cup (90 g) brown sugar

¼ cup (50 g) granulated sugar

½ cup (113 g) unsalted butter, melted

PAIRS WITH

Vanilla Bean Ice Cream (page 279)

Makes

1

10-INCH ROUND TART

SPRING

Rhubarb Curd Pie *with*
WHIPPED STRAWBERRY GANACHE

This creamy, curd-based twist on the popular spring pairing of strawberry and rhubarb makes a sweet and tart beauty. Use a pastry bag with a large star tip to create a beautiful top with the strawberry ganache, and garnish with fresh strawberries and Toffee Pecans for a lovely finish.

Preheat oven to 350°F. Press the crust into a deep-dish pie plate and bake for 6 minutes. Allow to cool.

To make the rhubarb curd: Add chopped rhubarb to a blender. Add lemon juice and blend until it turns to pulp. You may have to stop the blender and scrape down its sides to get all of the rhubarb to blend. Place a fine mesh sieve over a medium bowl. Pour the rhubarb pulp into the sieve, using a rubber spatula to get all of the pulp and juice. Push pulp into the sieve to squeeze out all of the juice. Juice should measure about ⅔ cup. It's okay if it's slightly under. Discard or repurpose any juice over ⅔ cup.

In a medium saucepan, whisk together sugar and cornstarch. Add the rhubarb juice and egg yolks and whisk until fully incorporated. Cook over medium-high heat, stirring constantly, until mixture becomes thick and coats the back of the spoon, 8 to 10 minutes. Use an instant read thermometer to check the temperature; it should reach 170°F. Transfer to the bowl of a stand mixer fitted with the paddle attachment. Mix on low. Add butter 1 teaspoon at a time, mixing until fully combined before adding the next teaspoon of butter. Strain through a sieve into a medium bowl. Pour while still warm into the pie crust. Cover with plastic wrap and refrigerate for at least 4 hours or overnight.

To make the whipped strawberry ganache: Add strawberries, sugar, and cornstarch to a blender. Blend until fully combined and strawberries are liquefied. Pour strawberry mixture into a saucepan. Cook over medium-high heat until thickened to the consistency of pudding. Remove from heat. Using a rubber spatula, pour and press the mixture through a fine mesh sieve. Stir in strawberry extract, if using. Set aside.

Deep-Dish Vanilla Wafer or Graham Cracker Crumb Crust (page 52)

RHUBARB CURD

4-5 stalks (300 g) rhubarb, chopped

2 tablespoons fresh lemon juice

¾ cup (150 g) sugar

3 tablespoons cornstarch

8 egg yolks

½ cup (113 g) unsalted butter

WHIPPED STRAWBERRY GANACHE

1½ cups (210 g) diced strawberries

2 tablespoons sugar

3 tablespoons cornstarch

½ teaspoon strawberry extract, optional

11 ounces (312 g) white chocolate, chopped

1½ cups heavy cream

2 teaspoons vanilla bean paste

2 drops pink food coloring gel

PAIRS WITH

Toffee Pecans (page 290)

Makes
1
DEEP-DISH PIE

SPRING

G✳F

page
95

Add white chocolate to a heatproof bowl. Add heavy cream, vanilla bean paste, and food coloring gel to a saucepan and heat over medium-high heat until steaming. Pour the mixture over the white chocolate and let it sit for about 1 minute. Using a rubber spatula, stir until chocolate is melted and combined. Add strawberry mixture and stir until smooth. Press plastic wrap directly onto the surface to prevent a skin from forming and refrigerate for 4 hours or overnight.

Add the set strawberry ganache to the bowl of a stand mixer fitted with the whisk attachment. Beat on high for about 5 minutes or until medium peaks form. Spread or pipe onto the cooled rhubarb curd. Serve immediately or cover and refrigerate until ready to serve.

Lemon Chess Pie

Chess pie is a sweet custard pie with a long history in the South. This citrusy, lemon twist on the classic is a bright, tart, and sweet treat that pairs perfectly with a big dollop of Whipped Cream. Decorate the top with a dusting of confectioners' sugar; this pretty, simple pie is a nice addition to an Easter gathering or spring potluck.

Parbake the crust in a 9-inch pie plate according to the instructions on page 41.

In the bowl of a stand mixer fitted with the paddle attachment, beat butter, sugar, and vanilla until light and fluffy, about 3 minutes. Add eggs one at a time, mixing between each addition. Add lemon juice and zest and mix until combined. In a small bowl, combine flour, cornmeal, and salt. Add to the butter mixture. Mix just until combined. Scrape the sides and bottom of the bowl to ensure even mixing. Pour into the prepared parbaked crust.

Bake at 425°F for 10 minutes. Reduce oven temperature to 300°F and bake for 40 additional minutes or until the center of the pie is only slightly jiggly. Allow the pie to cool completely before cutting. Dust with confectioners' sugar and serve with Whipped Cream.

Single Butter Pie Dough
(page 33)

FILLING
½ cup (113 g) unsalted butter
1¾ cups (350 g) granulated sugar
1 teaspoon vanilla extract
4 eggs, room temperature
½ cup fresh lemon juice
zest from 1 lemon
2 tablespoons all-purpose flour
1 tablespoon fine cornmeal
½ teaspoon fine sea salt

TO GARNISH
confectioners' sugar
Whipped Cream (page 276)

PAIRS WITH

Whipped Cream
(page 276)

Makes
1
CLASSIC-
SIZED PIE

SPRING

Asparagus *and* Gouda Galette

Asparagus is one of the earliest local crops to start appearing in markets and stores in my area in the spring. After a long winter, it's always a welcome sign to see that a bountiful summer of fresh produce is about to begin. This galette makes a cheerful, delicious side dish for a Mother's Day meal or any spring table.

Single Butter Pie Dough
(page 33)

1 pound (454 g) asparagus

2 tablespoons heavy cream

1 egg

1 clove garlic, minced

2 teaspoons chopped fresh chives

½ teaspoon red pepper flakes

5 ounces (142 g) Gouda cheese, shredded

2 tablespoons olive oil

fine sea salt and pepper, to taste

Egg Wash (page 275)

¼ cup (28 g) Parmesan, shredded

Preheat oven to 375°F. Line a half-sheet baking pan with a silicone baking mat or parchment paper.

Trim and wash asparagus and cut into bite-sized pieces. Allow to dry on a paper towel.

In a medium bowl, whisk egg and cream until fully incorporated. Add garlic, chives, and red pepper flakes and stir until combined. Add Gouda and stir until the cheese is evenly coated. Set aside.

In a medium bowl, add asparagus, olive oil, and salt and pepper to taste.

Roll out the dough on a lightly floured surface to roughly a 15-inch round. Wrap loosely around the rolling pin and transfer to the prepared baking sheet. Spread the cheese mixture evenly in the center of the crust, leaving a 2- to 3-inch border around the edge. Layer asparagus pieces on top of cheese. Fold border of the dough up and over, partially overlapping the filling. Pinch dough where it overlaps itself to seal in the filling and prevent leaks. Brush dough with Egg Wash. Sprinkle the entire top of the galette with Parmesan. Bake for 40 to 45 minutes or until the crust is golden brown. Serve warm.

Croque Madame Galette

I tried my first Croque Madame open-faced sandwich in one of my most-frequented lunch spots near Union Square, and I was instantly in love. Even though I am usually not a huge fan of ham, the balance of flavors with the mornay sauce and the bubbling, golden gruyère, topped with a fried egg, made for a delectable lunch. This version in galette form is equally delicious and makes a great addition to a brunch spread for a baby shower or Mother's Day meal. The colors of the bright yellow-orange yolks and sprinkle of fresh green parsley will brighten your spring table.

Preheat oven to 375°F. Line a half-sheet baking pan with a silicone baking mat or parchment paper.

To make the mornay sauce: Melt butter over medium-high heat in a skillet. Sprinkle flour over melted butter and whisk until a paste forms. Cook for about 2 minutes, continuously scraping the bottom of the skillet. Pour milk into the skillet and whisk until it fully incorporates. At first the mixture will be lumpy, but it will come together in a minute or two. Continue cooking and stirring until the mixture thickens. Add gruyère, Dijon mustard, and salt and pepper. Stir until the cheese has fully melted and is incorporated into the sauce. Remove from heat.

To assemble galette: Roll out dough on a lightly floured surface to roughly a 15-inch round. Wrap loosely around the rolling pin and transfer to the prepared baking sheet. Add some mornay sauce to the center of the dough, leaving a 2- to 3-inch border around the edge. Add a layer of ham slices and top with more sauce. Repeat until all of the ham and sauce are on the dough. Fold border of the dough up and over, partially overlapping the filling. Pinch dough where it overlaps itself to seal in the filling and prevent leaks. Brush Egg Wash on the dough. Bake for 20 minutes, then remove from oven and carefully sprinkle 2 ounces of shredded gruyère on top of the filling. Bake an additional 20 to 25 minutes or until the crust is golden brown and cheese is bubbling and lightly browned.

To fry the eggs: Preheat skillet over medium-high heat for 2 to 3 minutes, then add butter. When butter is melted and bubbling, crack eggs into the pan. Add salt and pepper to taste. Cover skillet and cook until egg whites have fully cooked but yolks are still runny, about 2 minutes. Add fried eggs to the top of the hot galette. Sprinkle with fresh parsley and serve immediately.

Single Butter Pie Dough
(page 33)

MORNAY SAUCE
¼ cup (56 g) salted butter

¼ cup (33 g) all-purpose flour

1 cup whole milk

2 ounces (57 g) gruyère, shredded

1 teaspoon Dijon mustard

fine sea salt and pepper, to taste

TO ASSEMBLE
7 ounces (198 g) thinly sliced precooked ham

2 ounces (57 g) gruyère, shredded

Egg Wash (page 275)

TOPPING
1 tablespoon salted butter

3 eggs

fine sea salt and pepper, to taste

1 tablespoon chopped fresh parsley

Makes
1
GALETTE

SPRING

page
101

Italian Easter Pie

After the lean times of Lent, some traditional Easter meals are especially rich–and this pie stuffed with a variety of meats and cheeses is no exception. Also known as pizza rustica, this Italian traditional pie is a great addition to a large Easter spread or can make a meal all on its own served up for Easter or for anytime you want to share a hearty meal.

Double Butter Pie Dough
(page 33)

1 pound (454 g) ground Italian sausage

2 cups (100 g) chopped fresh spinach, packed

4 ounces (113 g) soppressata

4 ounces (113 g) Genoa salami

4 ounces (113 g) pepperoni

8 ounces (227 g) fresh mozzarella

8 ounces (227 g) whole milk ricotta

8 ounces (227 g) basket cheese (or more ricotta)

4 ounces (113 g) shredded provolone

5 eggs

2 tablespoons heavy cream

freshly ground black pepper, to taste

Egg Wash (page 275)

Preheat oven to 375°F. Divide double pie dough, reserving ⅓ of the dough for the top crust and ⅔ for the bottom crust. On a lightly floured surface, roll out the larger portion of dough to a roughly 17-inch circle. Wrap loosely around the rolling pin and carefully place in a 9-inch springform pan, covering the bottom and sides. Take care not to puncture the dough, which can cause leaking while the filling bakes. Loosely cover with plastic wrap and place in the refrigerator while making the filling.

Brown the ground sausage. Remove from heat and add spinach immediately, when the sausage and pan are still hot. Stir until the spinach is incorporated and mostly wilted. Transfer to a large mixing bowl. Chop soppressata, Genoa salami, pepperoni, and fresh mozzarella into bite-sized pieces. Add to the mixing bowl. Add ricotta, basket cheese (if using), and provolone. Stir the mixture until ingredients are evenly distributed. Pour into the chilled crust. Place the pan on a rimmed baking sheet to catch any leaks while baking.

In the bowl of a stand mixer fitted with the whisk attachment, beat eggs, heavy cream, and pepper on high until light and foamy, about 3 minutes. Pour over the filling. On a lightly floured surface, roll out the remaining dough portion to roughly a 10-inch round. Add to the top of the pie. Pinch together the bottom and top crusts, and crimp. With a sharp knife, make 5 or 6 cuts in the top crust to vent. Generously brush with Egg Wash.

Bake for 1 hour and 10 minutes or until the top is golden brown and the filling is cooked all the way through. Remove the sides of the springform pan and serve hot.

❋ *This pie is traditionally served cold, but I think it is better served warm. The choice is yours!*

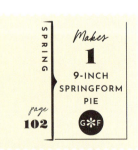

SPRING

Makes

1

9-INCH
SPRINGFORM
PIE

G❋F

Pasties

Pasties originated hundreds of years ago in Cornwall, England, but the Upper Peninsula of my home state, Michigan, now claims them as their own. In the 1800s, Cornish workers came to the area to mine copper, and they brought their love for these handheld meat and potato pies with them. You will find these steaming savory treats across the U.P. with a variety of fillings and accompaniments.

Preheat oven to 350°F. Line two baking sheets with parchment paper or silicone baking mats.

In a medium bowl, combine potatoes, rutabaga, onion, thyme, parsley, and salt and pepper. Stir to combine. In a separate medium bowl, crumble ground beef and add salt and pepper to taste.

Divide dough evenly into 8 balls. On a lightly floured surface, roll out each to a round about ⅛-inch thick. Place 4 dough rounds on each prepared pan. Place about ¼ cup of the vegetable mixture on one half of each dough round. Top each with 1 teaspoon of butter. Crumble 2 ounces ground beef over the top of the vegetables. Fold dough over the filling and crimp edges to seal. Make 2 to 3 cuts in the top crust of each pasty and generously brush with Egg Wash. Bake for about 40 to 45 minutes or until the tops are golden and the ground beef has cooked through. Serve hot with your choice of condiments.

Extra-Large Butter Pie Dough (page 33)

1½ cups (195 g) cubed Yukon potatoes

½ cup (85 g) cubed rutabaga

½ cup (63 g) diced onions

1 tablespoon fresh thyme leaves

2 tablespoons chopped fresh parsley

½ teaspoon fine sea salt

½ teaspoon freshly ground black pepper

1 pound (454 g) 85/15 ground beef

8 teaspoons salted butter

Egg Wash (page 275)

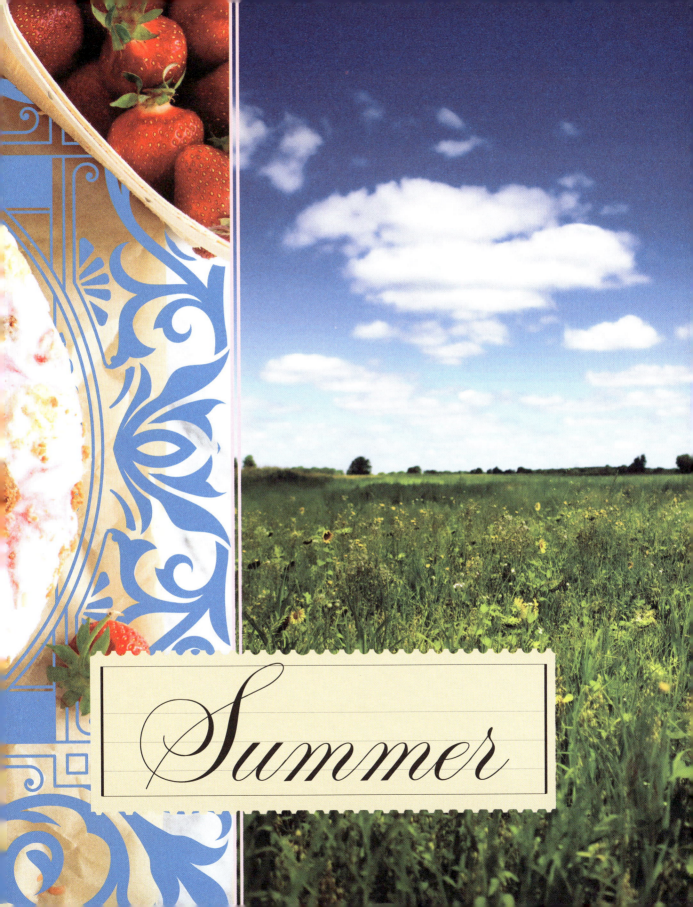

Summer

Angel Strawberry Pie

Similar to a pavlova, angel pies use a meringue crust and light, fluffy filling. This strawberry version has a sweet and creamy filling with a lovely crunch in the airy crust. Garnish with strawberry sauce and sliced berries for a lovely pink and red presentation.

Preheat oven to 200°F. Spray a deep-dish pie plate with nonstick spray and line a baking sheet with parchment paper and set aside. Prepare a large pastry bag with a large star or round tip and prop it in a tall glass. Fold over the top 2 to 3 inches of the opening so it is ready to be filled.

In the bowl of a stand mixer fitted with the whisk attachment, beat egg whites and cream of tartar at medium-low until foamy. Increase speed to medium and add sugar and confectioners' sugar slowly, 1 teaspoon at a time. Increase speed to medium-high for 2 minutes. Increase again to high speed, and continue to beat until stiff peaks form, about 3 to 4 additional minutes. Add vanilla extract and mix just until combined.

With a rubber spatula, scoop about ¾ of the meringue into the prepared pie plate and spread to cover bottom and sides of dish while leaving space for filling.

Add the remaining meringue to the prepared pastry bag. Pipe small star shapes onto the prepared baking sheet. Meringues do not expand like other cookies, so it's okay to space them close together. Bake meringue crust and mini meringue stars for at least 2 hours. After 2 hours, turn off the oven and leave them in the oven for another hour. The meringue should look dry when it is ready. Allow meringue to cool completely.

To make the filling: Wash and hull strawberries. In a medium bowl, smash berries with a potato masher. Set a fine mesh sieve over a medium bowl and pour smashed berries into the sieve to drain. In the bowl of a stand mixer, beat the cream cheese until fluffy, about 4 minutes. Add the heavy cream, confectioners' sugar, and vanilla extract and beat on high until stiff peaks form. Remove from the stand mixer and fold in drained strawberries with a rubber spatula, taking care not to deflate whipped cream. Add to the prepared meringue crust just before serving.

(continued)

MERINGUE CRUST

5 egg whites

¼ teaspoon cream of tartar

¾ cup (150 g) sugar

⅓ cup (36 g) confectioners' sugar

1 teaspoon vanilla extract

FILLING

1 pint (300 g) strawberries

8 ounces (227 g) cold cream cheese

1½ cups heavy cream

2 teaspoons vanilla extract

¾ cup (83 g) confectioners' sugar

STRAWBERRY SAUCE

1 pint (300 g) strawberries

3 tablespoons sugar

Makes
1
DEEP-DISH PIE

G✻F

SUMMER

page
109

To make the strawberry sauce: Wash and hull strawberries and place them in a 9 × 13 inch pan. Sprinkle the sugar over the berries, then mash with a potato masher. There should still be some chunks of berries left in the sauce. Top pie with strawberry sauce, garnish with meringue stars, and serve. Pie is best fresh.

❋ *Humidity can ruin meringue, making it sticky and chewy. If your house is humid, store meringue in an airtight container in the freezer until ready to use. Allow to thaw for 30 minutes outside of the container before adding the pie filling.*

TIPS FOR SUCCESSFUL MERINGUE

Getting your meringue into form for elegant piping and fluffy whisps requires achieving stiff peaks through extended whipping with a whisk beater. When the meringue holds its form on the end of the whisk, it is ready. Sometimes getting this just right is easier said than done. Here are a few tips to ensure meringue success.

❋ Protein is the building block for light, airy meringue. Any fat in the mix will prevent the protein bonds from forming properly and will deflate the meringue or keep it from ever reaching stiff peaks. To keep fat out, make sure your bowl and whisk are clean and dry. Also take care that yolks do not break while separating the eggs. Any yolk in the egg whites can make your meringue collapse.

❋ Cream of tartar is not an essential ingredient in meringue, but it will aid in the stability and speed of reaching the right consistency. The acidity in cream of tartar helps keep the protein molecules from sticking together, allowing the air bubbles to form and keeping them from deflating.

❋ Take care not to under- or over-beat your meringue. Reaching stiff peaks requires time and a high speed on your mixer to get the air into the meringue. You can also take it too far, making the meringue grainy or lumpy. Keep an eye on your meringue and stop mixing as soon as stiff peaks form.

Fresh Strawberry
OR PEACH Icebox Pie

My mom made a version of this pie every summer, and it was a family hit. I love strawberries and peaches unbaked, and this icebox pie balances these beautiful seasonal fruits in a sweet gelatin filling that goes perfectly in a crumb crust with a large dollop of Cream Cheese Whipped Cream.

Preheat oven to 350°F. Press crust into a deep-dish pie plate and bake for 6 minutes. Allow to cool.

Mix gelatin and water in a medium bowl and allow to bloom for 5 to 10 minutes.

Add 2 cups (300 g) strawberries to a blender with sugar and cornstarch. Blend on high until strawberries are completely liquefied. Pour into a saucepan and cook over medium-high heat, stirring constantly, until mixture begins to bubble. Remove from heat and add bloomed gelatin. Stir until completely incorporated. Allow the mixture to cool until just warm. Do not allow it to sit too long, or it will begin to solidify.

Slice remaining strawberries (900 g) and place in a large bowl. Pour cooled strawberry gelatin mixture over the sliced berries and stir to evenly coat. Pour into the cooled crust. Cover and refrigerate at least 2 hours or overnight. Serve with Cream Cheese Whipped Cream and Toffee Pecans.

Deep-Dish Vanilla Wafer or Graham Cracker Crumb Crust (page 52)

4 teaspoons gelatin

⅓ cup cold water

6½ cups (1.2 kg) fresh hulled strawberries, divided (or peeled, pitted, and sliced peaches)

1¼ cups (250 g) sugar

2 tablespoons cornstarch

PAIRS WITH

Cream Cheese Whipped Cream (page 277)

Toffee Pecans (page 290)

Makes
1
DEEP-DISH PIE

SUMMER

page
111

Strawberry Cheesecake Ice Cream Pie

This fabulous ice cream pie is loaded with rich, complex flavors. There are more steps in this recipe than most, but I promise each step is doable, and the end result is an ice cream pie as amazing as a New York cheesecake meeting a hand-dipped homemade strawberry ice cream cone. When strawberries are in season in early summer is the best time to enjoy this showstopper.

In a small bowl, combine ¼ cup milk with cornstarch. Mix until all lumps have dissolved. In a medium to large saucepan over medium-high heat, whisk together remaining milk, heavy cream, sugar, and malt powder. Add cornstarch slurry to saucepan and whisk to combine. On a cutting board with a sharp knife, cut open vanilla bean lengthwise. Using the edge of the knife, scrape the seeds from the vanilla bean and add to the milk mixture.

Continue cooking over medium-high heat until the mixture just about reaches a boil. Reduce heat to medium-low and continue cooking until it thickens slightly, about 5 more minutes. Allow to cool and then cover and chill in the refrigerator for at least 2 hours or overnight.

To make the mini cheesecakes: Preheat oven to 350°F. Spray three 4-inch ramekins with nonstick spray and set on a baking sheet. In a medium bowl, combine crust ingredients. Evenly divide the crust crumbs between the three ramekins. Press the crumbs into the bottom and partway up the sides of each ramekin.

In the bowl of a stand mixer fitted with the paddle attachment, beat cream cheese, butter, and sugar until light and fluffy, about 5 minutes. Add egg, buttermilk, flour, and vanilla extract, beating until fully combined and there are no lumps. Pour into ramekins and bake for 30 minutes. Cool completely and refrigerate for 1 hour. Chop 2 of the mini cheesecakes into bite-sized pieces, cover, and return to the refrigerator. (Consider the extra mini-cheesecake a baker's bonus—or reserve it in the refrigerator and garnish the finished pie with cheesecake pieces.)

(continued)

SPECIAL EQUIPMENT
Ice Cream Maker

Classic Graham Cracker Crumb Crust (page 52)

VANILLA BEAN ICE CREAM
1¾ cups whole milk, divided

2 tablespoons cornstarch

1¾ cups heavy cream

⅔ cup (132 g) sugar

¼ cup (35 g) malt powder

1 vanilla bean

MINI CHEESECAKE CRUSTS
¾ cup (85 g) graham cracker crumbs

1 tablespoon sugar

2½ tablespoons (35 g) unsalted butter, melted

MINI CHEESECAKE FILLING
8 ounces (227 g) cream cheese, softened

2 teaspoons unsalted butter, softened

PAIRS WITH

Toffee Pecans
(page 290)

Makes

1

CLASSIC-SIZED PIE

SUMMER

⅓ cup (66 g) sugar

1 egg, room temperature

¼ cup buttermilk

1 tablespoon all-purpose flour

1 teaspoon vanilla extract

STRAWBERRY SAUCE

4 cups (600 g) strawberries

⅓ cup (66 g) sugar

To make the crust: Preheat oven to 350°F. Press crumb crust into a 9-inch pie plate and bake for 6 minutes. If crust slips down the sides of the pan while baking, use a tamper or the back of a spoon to press the crust back up the sides of the pan. Allow to cool completely.

To make the ice cream: Add chilled cream mixture to ice cream maker and follow manufacturer's instructions to churn into ice cream.

While ice cream is churning, make the strawberry sauce: Wash and hull strawberries. Add them to a 9 × 13 inch pan. Sprinkle the sugar over the berries and mash with a potato masher. There should still be some chunks of berries in the sauce.

When ice cream is finished, scoop half into prepared pie crust. Add a layer of cheesecake pieces and strawberry sauce. Add the rest of the ice cream, then top with more cheesecake pieces and sauce. Keep remaining strawberry sauce for serving. Cover and freeze for at least 2 hours or overnight. When ready to serve, garnish with more sauce and reserved mini cheesecake pieces, if desired.

❊ *One of the easiest ways to cut this pie is to pop it out of the pie plate, place pie on a cutting board, and cut with a large chef's knife. Serve cut pieces immediately or return them to pie plate, cover, and store in the freezer.*

You can save time by purchasing a small vanilla cheesecake instead of making the homemade mini cheesecakes and/or using storebought vanilla ice cream.

Strawberries *and* Cream Tart

This icebox tart is based on my Aunt Judy's go-to summer strawberry recipe, which was the dessert I most hoped would show up at family gatherings when I was a kid. It marries a creamy layer with sweet fresh berries on top of a rich shortbread crust. In-season berries make it even more irresistible. This one never lasts long at our house.

Press-In Shortbread Tart Dough (page 49)

CREAM LAYER

8 ounces (227 g) cold cream cheese

⅔ cup (158 ml) heavy cream

1 tablespoon vanilla bean paste

⅔ cup (55 g) confectioners' sugar

STRAWBERRY LAYER

1½ cups (210 g) hulled strawberries

1 tablespoon cornstarch

¾ cup (150 g) sugar

1 pound (454 g) hulled strawberries, sliced

To make the crust: Preheat oven to 350°F. Press tart dough into a 10-inch tart pan. Generously dock the crust with a fork and bake for 25 to 30 minutes or until the crust is lightly golden. While still hot, use a tamper or the back of a spoon to lightly press down the center of the crust, leaving a ¾-inch border around the edge.

To make the cream layer: In the bowl of a stand mixer fitted with the whisk attachment, add cream cheese and heavy cream. Beat on medium speed for 4 to 5 minutes or until stiff peaks form. Add vanilla bean paste and confectioners' sugar. Mix until combined. Cover and refrigerate until ready to use.

To make the strawberry layer: Place 1½ cups strawberries, cornstarch, and sugar in a blender. Blend until strawberries are completely puréed. Pour mixture into a medium saucepan and cook over medium-high heat, stirring continuously, until mixture thickens and coats the back of the spoon, about 5 minutes. Remove from heat and allow to cool for about 15 minutes or until cool enough to touch.

Spread the cream layer into the cooled tart crust. Gently mix sliced strawberries into the cooled strawberry purée and stir to coat. Layer on top of cream. Cover and refrigerate for at least 1 hour, until set. Remove from tart pan and serve cold, garnished with Toffee Walnuts.

SUMMER

Makes

1

10-INCH TART

G✳F

PAIRS WITH

Toffee Walnuts
(variation; page 290)

Red, White, and Blue Tart

Here's a simple, lemony, refreshing summer fruit tart that's perfect for a Fourth of July picnic or cookout. It's pretty on any festive table spread and a tasty summer dessert.

To make the crust: Preheat oven to 350°F. Press tart dough into a 10-inch tart pan. Generously dock with a fork and bake for 25 to 30 minutes or until the crust is lightly golden. While still hot, use a tamper or the back of a spoon to lightly press down the center of the crust, leaving a ¾-inch edge.

To make the filling: In the bowl of a stand mixer fitted with the whisk attachment, beat cream cheese until fluffy, about 4 minutes. Add lemon juice, zest, vanilla extract, and confectioners' sugar and beat on high until fully combined and smooth. Add heavy cream and beat on high until stiff peaks form. Spread in the cooled tart crust and top with berries.

To make the glaze: In a small saucepan, whisk together lemon juice, sugar, and cornstarch. Cook over medium-high heat until mixture begins to bubble. Continue cooking and stirring until mixture thickens and coats the back of a spoon. Remove from heat and allow to cool for about 5 minutes. Do not cool completely, or it will become too thick to add to the tart evenly. With a pastry brush, coat berries with warm glaze. Refrigerate for at least an hour before removing from the tart pan and serving.

Press-In Shortbread Tart Dough (page 49)

FILLING

4 ounces (114 g) cold cream cheese

1 tablespoon fresh lemon juice

zest of half a lemon

1 teaspoon vanilla

½ cup (55 g) confectioners' sugar

1 cup heavy cream

FRUIT

1 pint (340 g) raspberries

1 pint (340 g) strawberries, hulled

1 pint (340 g) blueberries

1 pint (340 g) blackberries

GLAZE

⅓ cup fresh lemon juice

½ cup (100 g) sugar

1 tablespoon cornstarch

Makes **1** 10-INCH TART

SUMMER

page **119**

Classic Cherry Pie

Cherry farms dot the drive through Old Mission Peninsula in Grand Traverse Bay in one of the most celebrated areas in the US for cherries. In the spring, the trees are flush with blossoms, and the blue waters of the bay paint a pastoral picture. In the summer, U-pick cherries, roadside farm stands, and a cherry festival bring tourists to the area to celebrate the juicy red fruit. This cherry pie recipe is an American classic and a must-have for summer celebrations.

Double Butter Pie Dough
(page 33)

1 cup (200 g) sugar

¼ cup (40 g) cornstarch

¼ teaspoon fine sea salt

½ teaspoon cinnamon

6 cups (975 g) fresh sweet
cherries, pitted

1 tablespoon vanilla bean paste

2 tablespoons salted butter

Sweet Egg Wash (page 275)

Preheat oven to 400°F.

To make the filling: In a medium bowl, whisk together sugar, cornstarch, salt, and cinnamon. In a large bowl, toss together cherries and vanilla bean paste. Add sugar mixture and stir until cherries are evenly coated.

Roll out the first disk of pie dough on a lightly floured surface to roughly a 15-inch round. Wrap loosely around the rolling pin and transfer to a 9-inch pie plate. Cut off any extra crust and pour in cherries. Roll out the second half of the dough and place on top of filling. Cut off any extra crust, attach top crust to the bottom crust, and crimp edges. Brush the top crust with Sweet Egg Wash and cut vents into the top of the crust.

Refrigerate for 20 minutes before baking. Bake for 10 minutes, then reduce oven temperature to 375°F and bake for an additional 40 to 50 minutes, or until the crust is golden brown and the filling is bubbly. Allow to cool for at least 30 minutes before cutting. Serve with Vanilla Bean Ice Cream.

SUMMER

Makes
1
CLASSIC-
SIZED PIE

PAIRS WITH

Vanilla Bean Ice
Cream (page 279)

Black Forest Pie

Black Forest cake was first made in the Black Forest region of Germany and featured a chocolate cake soaked in kirsch and topped with cherries and whipped cream. This pie version of the renowned cake features all the flavors with a creamy, chocolatey filling topped with a cherry pie filling and Whipped Cream. Garnish with fresh cherries for a sweet presentation.

Blind-bake the crust in a deep-dish pie plate according to the instructions on page 41.

To make the chocolate cream filling: Place chopped chocolate in a heatproof bowl. Place a fine mesh sieve over the bowl and set aside. Mix about 2 tablespoons half and half with the cornstarch in a small bowl to make a slurry. In a medium saucepan, whisk together egg yolks, sugar, and the remainder of the half and half. Add the cornstarch slurry and whisk to combine. Cook over medium-high heat, stirring constantly, until mixture becomes thick and coats the back of the spoon, 8 to 10 minutes. Use an instant read thermometer to check the temperature; it should reach 170°F. Pour hot mixture into the sieve directly onto chocolate. Press mixture through the sieve. Allow hot mixture to sit for about 1 minute, then stir with a rubber spatula until chocolate has melted and is completely incorporated. Allow mixture to cool for a few more minutes until it is only warm.

In the bowl of a stand mixer fitted with the paddle attachment, beat butter, cocoa, vanilla extract, and salt on high until light and fluffy, about 5 minutes. Add cooled chocolate mixture and beat on high for 5 additional minutes, stopping once to scrape down the sides and bottom of the bowl to ensure even mixing. Spread chocolate cream over crust. Cover with plastic wrap and refrigerate for 1 hour.

To make the cherry filling: In a medium saucepan, combine all of the filling ingredients and cook over medium-high heat, stirring frequently, until cherries have partially broken down and mixture has thickened, about 7 to 9 minutes. Allow to cool to room temperature, then add to the top of the chocolate filling. Cover and refrigerate for at least 2 hours or overnight. Just before serving, top with fresh cherries, Whipped Cream, and Chocolate Curls.

Single Chocolate Pie Dough (page 35)

CHOCOLATE CREAM FILLING

5 ounces (142 g) dark chocolate, chopped

1 cup half and half, divided

2 tablespoons cornstarch

3 egg yolks

¾ cup (150 g) sugar

¼ cup (56 g) unsalted butter, room temperature

¼ cup (23 g) unsweetened cocoa powder

2 teaspoons vanilla extract

¼ teaspoon fine sea salt

CHERRY FILLING

½ cup (100 g) sugar

3 tablespoons cornstarch

3 cups (490 g) pitted fresh sweet cherries

2 tablespoons fresh lemon juice

3 tablespoons kirsch, optional

1 teaspoon vanilla extract

TO GARNISH

8-10 fresh sweet cherries with stems

Whipped Cream (page 276)

Chocolate Curls (page 293)

PAIRS WITH

Whipped Cream (page 276)

Dark Chocolate Curls (page 293)

Makes
1
DEEP-DISH PIE

S U M M E R

G✳F

Cherry Raspberry Crumble Slab Pie

Slab pies get their name from their flat, rectangular shape. Baked on a jelly roll pan or other rimmed baking sheet, they have a nice crust-to-filling ratio and are perfect for a crowd. This delicious pie bubbling with red, sweet fruit and topped with a buttery crumble is the perfect addition to a Fourth of July spread or any summer cookout. Serve warm with ice cream for the perfect treat on a hot day.

Extra-Large Butter Pie Dough (page 33)

FILLING

4 cups (650 g) pitted fresh sweet cherries

3 cups (375 g) raspberries

1 tablespoon fresh lemon juice

2 teaspoons vanilla bean paste

½ cup (100 g) sugar

¼ cup (40 g) cornstarch

CRUMBLE

1 cup (180 g) brown sugar

2 cups (260 g) all-purpose flour

1 cup (80 g) old-fashioned oatmeal

1 teaspoon cinnamon

½ teaspoon fine sea salt

1 cup (225 g) unsalted butter, melted

Preheat oven to 375°F. Set out a half-sheet baking pan (or jelly roll pan) with a 1-inch rim.

To prepare the crust: Divide the dough in two equal parts. On a lightly floured surface, roll out each portion roughly to a 15 × 10-inch rectangle. Wrap each half loosely around the rolling pin and transfer to the baking sheet, overlapping slightly and pressing down the middle seam to seal. The two dough rectangles should cover the full pan and go up the sides and just past the rim. Trim extra crust and crimp edges.

To make the filling: In a mixing bowl, combine cherries and raspberries. Add lemon juice and vanilla bean paste and toss to combine. In a small bowl, whisk together sugar and cornstarch and add to the fruit mixture. Pour evenly onto the crust.

To make the crumble: In a medium bowl, combine brown sugar, flour, oatmeal, cinnamon, and salt. Pour melted butter over the dry ingredients and stir until combined. Crumble over the fruit.

Bake for 45 minutes or until the top is golden brown and the filling is bubbling. Serve warm with Vanilla Bean Ice Cream.

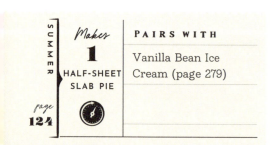

SUMMER

Makes

1

HALF-SHEET SLAB PIE

PAIRS WITH

Vanilla Bean Ice Cream (page 279)

Pistachio and Rose Tart

This tart was inspired by the flavors of nankhatai—my favorite South Asian cookie, which my friend Mumtaz shared with me years ago. Pistachios, rosewater, and cardamom create a unique flavor profile and a lovely pink dessert for a tea party or wedding shower.

To make the pistachio crust: Preheat oven to 350°F. In the bowl of a stand mixer fitted with the paddle attachment, beat the butter, vanilla extract, and confectioners' sugar until well combined, about 3 minutes. In a small bowl, combine flour, salt, and pistachios. Add to the butter mixture and mix until combined. Press dough into a 10-inch tart pan. Bake for 25 to 30 minutes or until crust is lightly golden. Cool completely.

To make the cream layer: In the bowl of a stand mixer fitted with the whisk attachment, add cream cheese and heavy cream. Beat on medium speed for 4 to 5 minutes or until soft peaks form. Add rosewater, cardamom, and confectioners' sugar. Mix until combined. Add to the cooled crust and spread evenly with an offset spatula. Refrigerate for 15 minutes.

To make the ganache: Add chopped white chocolate to a heatproof bowl. Whisk together heavy cream and pink food gel in a small saucepan. Cook over medium-high heat until steaming but not boiling. Remove from heat. Pour cream over chocolate and allow to sit for about 1 minute. Using a rubber spatula, stir until chocolate is melted and completely combined. Allow ganache to sit for 5 to 10 minutes until it thickens a little and pour over cooled tart. Cover and refrigerate for 1 hour or until ganache sets. Keep in the refrigerator until ready to serve.

To serve: Garnish with chopped pistachios, Sugared Rose Petals, and White Chocolate Curls.

PISTACHIO CRUST
¾ cup (169 g) unsalted butter, softened

2 teaspoons vanilla extract

⅔ cup (73 g) confectioners' sugar

1¾ cups (202 g) pastry or cake flour

½ teaspoon fine sea salt

½ cup (60 g) finely chopped pistachios

CREAM
4 ounces (227 g) cold cream cheese

⅔ cup (158 ml) heavy cream

½ teaspoon rosewater

½ teaspoon ground cardamom

⅔ cup (73 g) confectioners' sugar

GANACHE
5 ounces (141 g) white chocolate, chopped

½ cup heavy cream

2 drops pink food gel

TO GARNISH
coarsely chopped pistachios

Sugared Rose Petals (page 285)

White Chocolate Curls (page 293)

PAIRS WITH

White Chocolate Curls (page 293)

Sugared Rose Petals (variation; page 285)

Makes

1

10-INCH TART

SUMMER

Mackinac Island Fudge Ice Cream Pie

Mackinac Island is an iconic Michigan summer destination. Growing up in the state meant occasional trips to the quaint, automobile-free island with its landmark Grand Hotel and historic downtown lined with bike rentals and fudge shops. The famous fudge from the island inspired ice cream makers to create a Mackinac Island Fudge flavor, which was my favorite ice cream to get on the boardwalk on summer vacations. My interpretation of this childhood ice cream classic tastes even better with homemade fudge, put together in pie form.

SPECIAL EQUIPMENT
Ice Cream Maker

Classic Chocolate Wafer Crumb Crust (page 52)

VANILLA BEAN ICE CREAM
1¾ cups whole milk, divided

2 tablespoons cornstarch

1¾ cups heavy cream

¾ cup (150 g) sugar

1 vanilla bean

CHOCOLATE FUDGE
3 ounces (85 g) bittersweet chocolate, chopped

1 cup heavy cream

2 tablespoons light corn syrup

2 tablespoons water

6 tablespoons (84 g) unsalted butter

¾ cup (150 g) sugar

¾ cup (135 g) dark brown sugar

To make the ice cream: In a small bowl, combine ¼ cup milk with cornstarch. Mix until all lumps have dissolved. In a medium to large saucepan over medium-high heat, whisk together remaining milk, heavy cream, and sugar. Add cornstarch slurry to saucepan and whisk to combine. On a cutting board with a sharp knife, cut open vanilla bean lengthwise. Using the edge of the knife, scrape the seeds from the vanilla bean and add to the milk mixture. Continue cooking over medium-high heat until the mixture just about reaches a boil. Reduce heat to medium-low and continue cooking until it thickens slightly, about 5 more minutes. Allow to cool and then cover and chill in the refrigerator for at least 2 hours or overnight. Add chilled cream mixture to ice cream maker and follow manufacturer's instructions to churn into ice cream.

To make the crust: Preheat oven to 350°F. Press crumb crust into a 9-inch pie plate and bake for 6 minutes. If crust slips down the sides of the pan while baking, use a tamper or the back of a spoon to press the crust back up the sides of the pan. Allow to cool completely.

To make the fudge: Line a 9 × 9 inch pan with parchment paper and set near the stove on a hot pad. Place your coarsely chopped chocolate near your stove. Clip a candy thermometer to a 5 quart or larger pot or Dutch oven. (While cooking, the mixture will bubble and increase in volume.) Add all ingredients to the pot except the vanilla bean and chocolate. On a cutting board with a sharp knife, cut open vanilla bean lengthwise. Using the edge of the knife, scrape the seeds from the vanilla bean and add to the pot. Over medium heat, whisk ingredients until combined. Increase heat to medium-high and continue to stir. Do not leave the pot

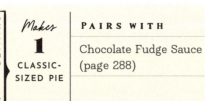

SUMMER

Makes
1
CLASSIC-
SIZED PIE

PAIRS WITH
Chocolate Fudge Sauce (page 288)

page
128

½ teaspoon fine sea salt

1 vanilla bean (or 1 tablespoon vanilla bean paste)

¾ cup Chocolate Fudge Sauce (page 288), plus more to garnish

unattended. If the mixture boils to near the top of the pot, reduce heat. Stir continuously until mixture reaches 230°F. Turn off heat and add chocolate, stirring until chocolate is melted and thoroughly combined. Work quickly—the fudge sets rapidly as it cools. Pour into the prepared pan. Allow to cool and set completely. Coarsely chop the cooled fudge.

To assemble the pie: Add a thin layer of Chocolate Fudge Sauce to the bottom of the pie crust. When ice cream is finished, scoop half into pie crust. Add a layer of chopped fudge. Add the rest of the ice cream and top with more fudge (reserve some to garnish), then add the remaining Chocolate Fudge Sauce. Swirl the fudge and Chocolate Fudge Sauce into the ice cream. Cover and freeze for at least 2 hours or overnight. When ready to serve, garnish with more Chocolate Fudge Sauce and reserved fudge.

Root Beer Float Pie

Modern root beer is based on a beverage in pre-colonial North America made from sassafras, which was later carbonated in Victorian-era soda fountains across the United States. Root beer floats are a foamy, cold American summer classic that I loved growing up. This sweet frozen treat captures the vintage soda flavors in pie form.

In a large pot, whisk together heavy cream and 1½ cups milk. In a small bowl, combine remaining ¼ cup milk with cornstarch. Mix until all lumps have dissolved and add to the pot. Add root beer syrup and vanilla bean paste and whisk to combine. Cook over medium-high heat until the mixture just about reaches a boil. Reduce heat to medium-low and continue cooking until it thickens, about 5 more minutes. Allow to cool and then cover and chill in the refrigerator for at least 2 hours or overnight.

To make the crust: Preheat oven to 350°F. Press crumb crust into a 9-inch pie plate and bake for 6 minutes. If the crust slips down the sides of the pan while baking, use a tamper or the back of a spoon to press the crust back up the sides of the pan. Allow to cool completely.

Add chilled cream mixture to an ice cream maker and follow the manufacturer's instructions to churn into ice cream. When ice cream is finished, scoop into the cooled crust. Cover and freeze for at least 2 hours or overnight. When ready to serve, garnish with maraschino cherries and Whipped Cream.

❋ *One of the easiest ways to cut this pie is to pop it out of the pie plate, place the pie on a cutting board, and cut with a large chef's knife. Serve cut pieces immediately or return them to pie plate, cover, and store in the freezer.*

SPECIAL EQUIPMENT
Ice Cream Maker

Classic Vanilla Wafer or Graham Cracker Crumb Crust (page 52)

ROOT BEER ICE CREAM
2 cups heavy cream

1¾ cups whole milk, divided

3 tablespoons cornstarch

1 cup root beer syrup (such as Torani)

1 tablespoon vanilla bean paste

TO GARNISH
12 maraschino cherries

Whipped Cream (page 276)

PAIRS WITH

Whipped Cream
(page 276)

Makes
1
CLASSIC-
SIZED PIE

SUMMER

Creamsicle Chiffon Pie

After years of baking and cooking for her family and friends, my mom has a lot of knowledge on what makes a crowd-pleaser. So I enlisted her to taste test pies, and this was one of her top choices. Chiffon pies were first created a century ago and have come in many varieties; this version celebrates the old favorite, orange and vanilla ice cream creamsicles, with a cream layer topped by orange chiffon.

Deep-Dish Vanilla Wafer or
Graham Cracker Crumb Crust
(page 52)

ORANGE CREAM

1 teaspoon unflavored gelatin

2 tablespoons cold water

½ cup fresh orange juice

zest of 2 oranges

½ cup sweetened condensed milk

4 ounces (114 g) cream cheese,
cold

1-2 drops orange food coloring

VANILLA CREAM LAYER

¾ cup heavy cream

4 ounces (114 g) cream cheese,
cold

¼ cup sweetened condensed milk

1 teaspoon vanilla extract

ORANGE CHIFFON

3 egg whites, from pasteurized
eggs (see note)

¼ cup (50 g) sugar

TO GARNISH

orange zest

Make orange cream in advance: In a small bowl, combine gelatin and water and allow to bloom (5 to 10 minutes). In a saucepan over medium heat, cook orange juice, zest, and sweetened condensed milk until steaming but not boiling. Remove from heat and whisk in bloomed gelatin. Allow to cool until it is just warm. In the bowl of a stand mixer, beat cream cheese and food coloring for 2 minutes. Add warm orange juice mixture and mix until fully incorporated. Cover and refrigerate at least 4 hours or overnight.

Preheat oven to 350°F. Press crust into a deep-dish pie plate and bake for 6 minutes. Allow to cool.

To make vanilla cream layer: In the bowl of a stand mixer fitted with the whisk attachment, beat heavy cream, cream cheese, sweetened condensed milk, and vanilla on high until light and smooth, about 5 minutes. With a rubber spatula, spread on the bottom of the pie crust.

To make orange chiffon layer: In the bowl of a stand mixer fitted with the whisk attachment, beat egg whites on medium speed until foamy. Increase the speed to high and slowly add sugar 1 teaspoon at a time. Beat until stiff peaks form. With a rubber spatula, carefully fold chilled orange cream into egg whites, taking care not to deflate the egg whites. Stir by hand just until combined. Pile on top of the vanilla cream layer and garnish with additional orange zest if desired. Serve immediately or cover and refrigerate until ready to serve.

SUMMER

Makes
1
DEEP-DISH
PIE

page
132

Pasteurization is a process of food preservation in which foods are treated with mild heat that either destroys or deactivates microorganisms and enzymes, including some bacteria, that contribute to food spoilage or the risk of disease. In other words, pasteurized eggs have been heated to a high enough temperature for a long enough time to kill salmonella, and are therefore safer to eat than other raw eggs.

Pink Lemonade Pie

This refreshing icebox pie is sweet-tart summer perfection. It elicits all the fond childhood memories of a cold glass of lemonade on a hot day. Garnish with Whipped Cream and lemon slices for a pretty pastel addition to a summer picnic spread or potluck.

Preheat oven to 350°F. Press crust into a deep-dish pie plate. Bake for 6 minutes. Allow to cool.

To make the lemon curd: Whisk together egg yolks, zest, lemon juice, and sugar in a saucepan. Cook over medium-high heat, stirring constantly, until mixture becomes thick and coats the back of the spoon, 8 to 10 minutes. Use an instant read thermometer to check the temperature; it should reach 170°F. Transfer to the bowl of a stand mixer fitted with the paddle attachment. Mix on low. Add butter 1 teaspoon at a time, mixing until fully combined before adding the next teaspoon of butter. Allow the mixer to run on low until the curd is no longer hot. Strain through a fine mesh sieve into a medium bowl. Press plastic wrap directly on the surface of curd to prevent a skin from forming. Refrigerate for at least 4 hours or overnight.

In the bowl of a stand mixer fitted with the whisk attachment, beat cream cheese until fluffy, about 4 minutes. Add heavy cream, confectioners' sugar, and vanilla extract and beat on high until stiff peaks form. Remove from the stand mixer and fold in the fully set lemon curd and pink food gel with a rubber spatula, taking care not to deflate whipped cream. Add to the prepared pie crust. Pipe Whipped Cream on top and garnish with lemon slices. Refrigerate for 1 hour before serving.

Deep-Dish Graham Cracker Crumb Crust (page 52)

LEMON CURD
5 egg yolks

zest of 2 lemons

⅓ cup fresh lemon juice

¾ cup (150 g) sugar

6 tablespoons (84 g) salted butter

FILLING
8 ounces (227 g) cold cream cheese

2½ cups heavy cream

2 teaspoons vanilla extract

½ cup (55 g) confectioners' sugar

2-3 drops pink food gel

TO GARNISH
Whipped Cream (page 276)

lemon slices

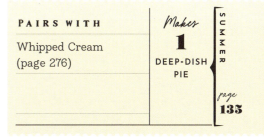

PAIRS WITH

Whipped Cream
(page 276)

Makes
1
DEEP-DISH
PIE

SUMMER

Mixed Fruit *and* Cream *Mini* Galettes

These delicious individual-sized galettes are fun for a party; they allow guests a choice of their favorite fruit version. You can even get all the parts together with a variety of fruits and allow guests to assemble their own galette. They taste best right out of the oven with a scoop of Vanilla Bean Ice Cream or fresh Whipped Cream.

Double Butter Pie Dough
(page 33)

CREAM FILLING

8 ounces (227 g) cream cheese, softened

¼ cup (50 g) sugar

1 egg

1 teaspoon vanilla extract

¼ cup (33 g) all-purpose flour

1 tablespoon cornstarch

¼ teaspoon fine sea salt

6 cups fresh fruit, such as berries, sliced stone fruit, or pitted tart cherries

2 tablespoons fresh lemon juice

½ cup (100 g) sugar

¼ cup cornstarch

1 teaspoon cinnamon

Egg Wash (page 275)

3 tablespoons turbinado sugar

Preheat oven to 375°F. Line two baking sheets with parchment paper or a silicone baking mat.

To make the cream filling: In the bowl of a stand mixer fitted with the paddle attachment, beat cream cheese, sugar, egg, and vanilla extract until smooth. In a small bowl, whisk together flour, cornstarch, and salt. Add to the cream cheese mixture. Beat until smooth.

To prepare the fruit: If using a variety of fruits, mix them or place them in separate bowls to make different varieties of mini galettes. Add lemon juice and toss to coat. In a small bowl, mix sugar, cornstarch, and cinnamon. Add to fruit and toss to coat.

To assemble: Divide crust dough into 12 equal pieces. Roll each out to a roughly 7-inch round. Place onto the prepared pans, 6 rounds per pan. Spread about 1 tablespoon of the cream cheese mixture in the center of each pie dough round, leaving a 1-inch border. Cover the cream with a layer of fruit, about ½ cup per galette. Fold the crust edges up and over and pinch seams.

Brush top crust with Egg Wash and sprinkle with turbinado sugar. Refrigerate for about 15 minutes before baking. Bake one pan at a time, for about 30 to 35 minutes or until golden brown. While the first pan bakes, store the second in the refrigerator. If any of the filling leaks out while baking, cut away and discard. Allow to cool on the pan for 5 minutes and serve warm with Whipped Cream or Vanilla Bean Ice Cream.

PAIRS WITH

Whipped Cream
(page 276)

Vanilla Bean Ice
Cream (page 279)

S'mores Tart

The gathering of friends and family around a fire while camping near Lake Michigan holds a dear spot in the memories of my youth. Nothing tasted better than hot, gooey s'mores eaten while sitting snugly by those cozy firepits. I love how this simple dessert can carry all that wistful sweetness tucked into a tart.

Preheat oven to 350°F. Press crust into a 10-inch tart pan and set aside.

To make the chocolate filling: In the bowl of a stand mixer fitted with the whisk attachment, beat eggs, sugar, vanilla, and salt on low for 5 minutes. In a medium saucepan over medium-high heat, heat heavy cream and butter until butter is melted and the mixture is steaming but not boiling. Remove from heat and add chopped chocolate. Whisk until chocolate has melted completely and is fully incorporated. With the mixer running on low, slowly and carefully pour the chocolate mixture into the egg mixture. Mix for an additional 3 to 5 minutes until fully incorporated and smooth.

Pour the filling into the prepared crust and bake for 20 to 25 minutes or until the filling has set at the edges but is still a bit jiggly in the center. Allow tart to cool completely.

To make the Swiss meringue: Whisk together egg whites and sugar in the top pan of a double boiler until completely incorporated. Cook, whisking continuously, until the mixture reaches 170°F, about 5 to 6 minutes. Pour into the bowl of a stand mixer fitted with the whisk attachment. Add cream of tartar. Beat on high for about 5 minutes. Add vanilla bean paste and continue to beat on high until stiff peaks form. Scoop or pipe onto cooled tart. Toast meringue with a kitchen torch or under an oven broiler. Keep a close watch on meringue while toasting to avoid burning. Remove from the tart pan and serve immediately, or store in the refrigerator until ready to eat.

Tart Graham Cracker Crumb Crust (page 52)

CHOCOLATE FILLING
3 eggs

½ cup (100 g) sugar

2 teaspoons vanilla extract

½ teaspoon fine sea salt

½ cup heavy cream

4 tablespoons (56 g) unsalted butter

6 ounces (170 g) semisweet chocolate, chopped

SWISS MERINGUE
4 egg whites

1 cup (200 g) sugar

½ teaspoon cream of tartar

1 teaspoon vanilla bean paste

Peach Galette

Peach season is a short but glorious time of the year in Michigan, and it's the only time I get to eat these juicy, sweet beauties. I never buy off-season peaches, which are usually mealy and have almost no scent or flavor. So when local peaches are available, I like to pick up a half bushel at an orchard or farmers' market. I bring out all my favorite peach recipes to take advantage of the small window of peachy deliciousness. This recipe is very simple and easy to throw together, and is the perfect summer flavor with tender, aromatic peaches and flaky just-from-the-oven crust. It reaches absolute perfection when topped with vanilla ice cream.

Single Butter Pie Dough
(page 33)

3 cups (675 g) sliced peaches

⅓ cup (66 g) sugar

2 teaspoons cornstarch

½ teaspoon cinnamon

1½ teaspoons vanilla bean paste

Egg Wash (page 275)

2 tablespoons turbinado sugar

Preheat oven to 375°F. Line a half-sheet pan with parchment paper or a silicone baking mat. Roll out pie dough to about a 15-inch round. Wrap dough loosely around the rolling pin and transfer to the prepared baking sheet.

Place a fine mesh sieve over a medium bowl. Add sliced peaches to sieve and allow to drain for 5 minutes, retaining the juice. In a small bowl, mix sugar, cornstarch, and cinnamon. Place drained peaches in a medium bowl. Sprinkle sugar mixture over peaches. Add vanilla bean paste and 2 tablespoons reserved peach juice. Stir until peaches are evenly coated.

Add peaches to the center of the prepared crust, leaving a 2- to 3-inch border. Fold edges of crust up and over, partially overlapping the filling. Pinch crust where it overlaps to seal in the filling and prevent leaks. Brush Egg Wash on top crust and sprinkle with turbinado sugar. Bake for 30 to 35 minutes or until the filling is bubbling and the top crust is golden brown. Allow to cool for 15 minutes and serve warm with Vanilla Bean Ice Cream.

SUMMER

Makes
1
GALETTE

PAIRS WITH

Vanilla Bean Ice
Cream (page 279)

Peaches *and* Cream Pie

Peaches have always paired beautifully with cream, whether ice cream or, in this case, cream cheese. With the crisp Oatmeal Cookie crust and the crunch of pecans in the crumb, this is bright and cheerful summer baked into a pie.

Preheat oven to 350°F. Press crust into a deep-dish pie plate and set aside.

To make the filling: Add sliced peaches to a fine mesh sieve set over a bowl. Squeeze lemon juice over peaches and stir to coat. Allow the juices to drain, retaining the juice.

In the bowl of a stand mixer fitted with the paddle attachment, beat cream cheese and sugar on medium speed until fluffy, about 3 minutes. Add eggs, 2 tablespoons reserved peach juice, heavy cream, and cornstarch. Beat on medium speed until batter is smooth, stopping to scrape the bottom and sides of the bowl to ensure even mixing. Remove bowl from stand mixer. Add the drained peaches and stir with a rubber spatula. Pour batter into the prepared crust.

To make the crumb: In a medium bowl, combine all of the dry ingredients. Pour the cooled butter over the dry ingredients and stir to combine. When the crumb starts to form, work with your hands until the ingredients are incorporated. Crumble over the peach mixture.

Bake for about 45 minutes, or until the center is only slightly jiggly and a cake tester inserted near the edge comes out clean. Allow to cool completely, then cover and refrigerate for at least 2 hours before cutting. Serve with Vanilla Bean Ice Cream.

Deep-Dish Oatmeal Cookie Crumb Crust (page 52)

FILLING
3 cups (575 g) peeled and sliced peaches

juice of half a lemon

8 ounces (227 g) cream cheese, softened

⅔ cup (132 g) sugar

2 teaspoons vanilla bean paste

2 eggs

¼ cup heavy cream

2 tablespoons cornstarch

PECAN CRUMB
½ cup (90 g) brown sugar

½ teaspoon fine sea salt

½ cup (50 g) coarsely chopped pecans

1 cup (130 g) all-purpose flour

6 tablespoons (84 g) unsalted butter, melted and cooled

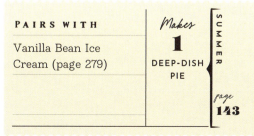

PAIRS WITH

Vanilla Bean Ice Cream (page 279)

Makes
1
DEEP-DISH PIE

SUMMER

page **143**

Peach Cobbler Slab Pie

Peach cobbler is a classic recipe first created by placing biscuit dough on top of sliced peaches and baking on an open hearth. The pairing has been popular ever since. In this version, the classic comes together as a slab pie, which makes a square of this cobbler tidy enough to hold in your hand as a snack. And, of course, it also tastes great warm in a bowl with a scoop of Vanilla Bean Ice Cream.

Extra-Large Butter Pie Dough (page 33)

PEACH FILLING

9 cups (1.5 kg) peeled and sliced peaches

1 tablespoon fresh lemon juice

2 teaspoons vanilla bean paste

½ cup (100 g) sugar

¼ cup (40 g) cornstarch

1 teaspoon cinnamon

¼ teaspoon nutmeg

COBBLER TOPPING

3 cups (345 g) self-rising flour (see note)

½ cup (100 g) sugar

½ teaspoon fine sea salt

6 tablespoons (84 g) unsalted butter

1½ cups heavy cream

Egg Wash (page 275)

3 tablespoons turbinado sugar

Preheat oven to 375°F. Set out a half-sheet pan (or jelly roll pan) with a 1-inch rim.

To prepare the crust: Divide the dough into two equal parts. On a lightly floured surface, roll out each portion roughly to a 15 × 10-inch rectangle. Wrap each half loosely around the rolling pin and place on the baking sheet, overlapping slightly and pressing down the middle seam to seal. The two dough rectangles should cover the full pan and go up the sides and just past the rim. Trim extra crust and crimp edges.

To make the filling: In a mixing bowl, combine peach slices, lemon juice, and vanilla bean paste. In a small bowl, whisk together sugar, cornstarch, cinnamon, and nutmeg. Add to the peaches and stir to evenly coat. Pour onto the crust.

To make the cobbler topping: In a medium bowl, combine self-rising flour, sugar, and salt. Slice butter into small pats and toss into the flour mixture. Cut butter into the flour mixture with a pastry blender until you have a coarse crumb. This step can also be achieved with a food processor or the pastry attachment of a stand mixer. Be careful not to overprocess; there should be some chunks of butter. Using a rubber spatula, stir in cream. When the liquid is mostly worked into the crumb, turn out onto a pastry board or countertop. Finish combining with your hands just until the dough holds together. Form ½-inch-thick patties and place on top of the peaches. With a pastry brush, top cobbler with Egg Wash and sprinkle turbinado sugar over the top. Bake for 45 to 50 minutes or until cobbler is golden brown and filling is bubbling. Serve warm with Vanilla Bean Ice Cream.

❋ *I prefer to use White Lily Self-Rising Flour in this recipe to create the soft, delicate rise of a Southern biscuit. This brand originated in the South and is milled from a soft red winter wheat that has a low protein content, which creates an airiness and pillow-like texture you can't achieve with all-purpose flour. If you don't have self-rising soft wheat flour on hand, you can substitute 3 cups cake flour, 1 tablespoon baking powder, and ½ teaspoon baking soda.*

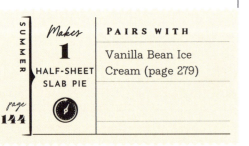

SUMMER

Makes
1
HALF-SHEET SLAB PIE

PAIRS WITH

Vanilla Bean Ice Cream (page 279)

Fresh Fig Galette *with*
MASCARPONE WHIPPED CREAM

Figs are an ancient fruit and have been an important part of Middle Eastern and Mediterranean cuisine for centuries. The fruit–which represents prosperity, blessings, and peace–is mentioned in the Bible frequently, representing how important this sweet, fragile fruit was in ancient times. The pairing of figs with honey is a quintessential combination from the region. Fresh figs can be tricky to find in modern US supermarkets, but when you spot some, this is a delicious way to prepare them. Topped with mascarpone whipped cream and drizzled with honey, this galette is a sweet summery presentation of one of earth's most ancient fruits.

¼ cup (30 g) chopped pistachios

Preheat oven to 375°F. Line a half-sheet pan with parchment paper or a silicone baking mat.

In a medium heatproof bowl, melt butter. Whisk in brown sugar, honey, salt, and cinnamon. With a sharp knife on a cutting board, cut vanilla bean lengthwise. Open the bean and scrape the seeds from the inside using the edge of the knife. Add seeds to the butter mixture. Whisk until seeds are evenly distributed. Set aside.

Roll out pie dough to about a 15-inch round. Wrap loosely around the rolling pin and transfer to the prepared baking sheet. Spread the butter mixture evenly across the crust, leaving a 2- to 3-inch border. Layer sliced figs over the butter mixture. Fold edges of crust up and over, partially overlapping the filling. Brush Egg Wash on top crust and sprinkle with turbinado sugar. Bake for 30 to 35 minutes or until filling is bubbling and top crust is golden brown. Allow to cool.

To make the mascarpone whipped cream: In the bowl of a stand mixer fitted with the whisk attachment, beat mascarpone, confectioners' sugar, and vanilla on medium speed until smooth and fluffy, about 4 minutes. Add heavy cream and beat on high until stiff peaks form, about 4 more minutes. Add to the top of the galette. Drizzle with honey, sprinkle with pistachios, and serve.

Single Butter Pie Dough
(page 33)

2 tablespoons unsalted butter

2 tablespoons brown sugar

2 tablespoons honey, plus more for serving

½ teaspoon fine sea salt

½ teaspoon cinnamon

1 vanilla bean

12 (500 g) fresh figs, sliced

Egg Wash (page 275)

2 tablespoons turbinado sugar

MASCARPONE WHIPPED CREAM

4 ounces (113 g) mascarpone cheese, cold

1 teaspoon vanilla extract

¾ cup (82 g) confectioners' sugar

1 cup heavy cream

TO GARNISH

honey

Makes
1
GALETTE

SUMMER

G✳F

page **147**

No-Churn Chocolate Malt Ice Cream Pie

If you don't have an ice cream maker but want to make an ice cream pie with homemade ice cream, here is a no-churn recipe you can try! My mom and my Aunt Judy used to work at a family drive-in restaurant where they served old-fashioned chocolate malts, and later, when they had kids, they would make them for us. This pie takes that flavor combination and adds malted milk balls for some crunch. Very sweet and chocolatey–this is a great summer treat.

Classic Chocolate Wafer Crumb Crust (page 52)

CHOCOLATE ICE CREAM FILLING

2 cups heavy cream

1 (14 ounce) can sweetened condensed milk

¼ cup Chocolate Fudge Sauce (page 288)

⅓ cup malt powder

¼ cup unsweetened cocoa powder

1 vanilla bean

1½ cups (200 g) chocolate-covered malted milk balls

TOPPING

3 ounces (85 g) semisweet chocolate, coarsely chopped

4 teaspoons coconut oil

Preheat oven to 350°F. Press crust into a 9-inch pie plate and bake for 6 minutes. Allow to cool.

In the bowl of a stand mixer fitted with the whisk attachment, beat heavy cream on high until stiff peaks form. Transfer to another bowl and set aside. Switch to the paddle attachment. Add sweetened condensed milk, Chocolate Fudge Sauce, malt powder, and unsweetened cocoa, and mix on medium speed until fully incorporated. Using a sharp knife, cut vanilla bean lengthwise on a cutting board. Open the bean and scrape out seeds and add to the bowl. Mix until incorporated.

Crush malted milk balls in a resealable bag (or chop) and set aside about ¼ cup to garnish. Add remaining crushed candy to the ice cream mixture. Remove bowl from stand mixer and fold whipped cream gently into mixture with a rubber spatula. Stir just enough to incorporate, taking care not to totally deflate heavy cream. Add to the prepared pie crust. The filling will mound a bit.

To make the topping: In a heatproof bowl, add chocolate and coconut oil. Microwave on low in 30-second intervals until chocolate has melted. Stir with a rubber spatula and drizzle over the ice cream mixture. Sprinkle with reserved crushed malted milk balls. Set in the freezer, uncovered, for about 10 minutes, or until the topping has set. Then cover with foil or plastic wrap and freeze for at least 3 hours before serving with additional Chocolate Fudge Sauce.

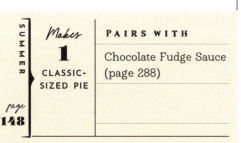

SUMMER

Makes
1
CLASSIC-SIZED PIE

PAIRS WITH

Chocolate Fudge Sauce (page 288)

Lemon Blueberry Cream Crumb Pie

Part cheesecake, part coffee cake, part pie, this amalgam of so many amazing desserts is one of my all-time favorites. Blueberries and lemons are such lovely, summery flavors–I promise this one will be a hit.

Preheat oven to 350°F. Press crust into a deep-dish pie plate and set aside.

To make the filling: In the bowl of a stand mixer fitted with the paddle attachment, beat cream cheese and sugar on medium speed until fluffy, about 3 minutes. Add eggs, lemon juice, buttermilk, flour, and lemon zest, and beat on medium speed until fully incorporated and batter is smooth. Scrape the bottom and sides of the bowl to ensure even mixing. Remove bowl from stand mixer. Add blueberries to batter and stir with a rubber spatula. Pour batter into prepared crust.

To make the crumb: In a medium bowl, whisk together all the dry ingredients. Pour melted butter over and mix with a rubber spatula or your hands until a crumb forms. Crumble chunks of crumb on top of blueberry batter. Bake for about 45 minutes, or until the center is only slightly jiggly and a cake tester inserted near the edge comes out clean. Allow to cool completely.

Garnish with Cream Cheese Whipped Cream and lemon zest. Serve immediately with Blueberry Sauce, if desired, or store in the refrigerator until ready to serve.

Deep-Dish Vanilla Wafer or Graham Cracker Crumb Crust (page 52)

FILLING

8 ounces (227 g) cream cheese, softened

½ cup (100 g) sugar

2 eggs, room temperature

¼ cup fresh lemon juice

¼ cup buttermilk

2 tablespoons all-purpose flour

zest of 1 lemon

2 cups (280 g) blueberries

CRUMB

1 cup (130 g) all-purpose flour

zest of one lemon

⅔ cup (132 g) sugar

½ cup (113 g) unsalted butter, melted

TO GARNISH

Cream Cheese Whipped Cream (page 277)

lemon zest

PAIRS WITH

Cream Cheese Whipped Cream (page 277)

Blueberry Sauce (page 287)

Makes
1
DEEP-DISH PIE

SUMMER

Caramelized Onion Goat Cheese Tart

When I told my boss and friend I was writing this book, she told me she had amazing memories of a caramelized onion and goat cheese tart she'd tried years before, and she encouraged me to come up with a recipe to match her memory. This savory tart makes a delicious side for a party or a family meal; the sweetness of the onions pairs nicely with the goat cheese and buttery fall-apart crust. This one's for you, Paula.

SAVORY TART CRUST

2 cups (260 g) all-purpose flour

½ teaspoon fine sea salt

½ cup (169 g) unsalted butter, softened

2 tablespoons olive oil

1 egg, room temperature

FILLING

2 tablespoons olive oil

1 tablespoon salted butter

5 cups (675 g) sliced sweet onions

1 tablespoon balsamic vinegar

fine sea salt and pepper to taste

2 eggs

½ cup heavy cream

5 ounces (142 g) goat cheese

2 teaspoons fresh thyme leaves, plus more to garnish

To make the crust: Preheat oven to 350°F. Whisk flour and salt together in a medium bowl. In the bowl of a stand mixer fitted with the paddle attachment, add butter, olive oil, and egg and mix until combined. Add the flour and mix on low until fully incorporated and a smooth dough forms. If dough is too sticky, cover with plastic wrap and refrigerate for 15 minutes. Press into the tart pan. Generously dock with a fork and parbake for 15 minutes.

To make the filling: Place olive oil and butter in a large skillet over medium heat. When butter is melted, add onions and sauté for 5 minutes, until onions have softened. Add balsamic vinegar and salt and pepper to taste. Reduce heat to medium-low and continue to cook, stirring every couple of minutes, until onions have caramelized and turned brown, about 20 to 30 minutes.

In a medium bowl, whisk eggs and heavy cream until fully combined. Break goat cheese into small pieces and add to the egg mixture. Add fresh thyme and stir.

Cover the bottom of the parbaked crust with about ¾ of the caramelized onions. Pour egg mixture over top, then evenly cover with remaining onions. Bake for 45 to 50 minutes or until the top is a deep golden brown. Garnish with fresh thyme and serve immediately.

SUMMER

Makes
1
10-INCH
TART

page
152

Heirloom Tomato *and* Burrata Galette

What could be better than fresh heirloom tomatoes with pesto and creamy burrata? This galette is perfection in the summer when basil is in abundance and tomatoes are ripening on the vine steps from your door. If you don't have your own garden, head to the farmers' market to get the freshest ingredients. This makes a great addition to an appetizer spread or a savory side for a summer potluck.

Preheat oven to 375°F. Line a half-sheet pan with a silicone baking mat or parchment paper.

To make the pesto: In the bowl of a food processor, coarsely chop pine nuts, garlic, salt, and pepper. Add basil and pulse until basil is finely chopped. Pour in olive oil while the food processor is running. Process until smooth. Add Parmesan and pulse to combine.

To assemble galette: Roll out dough on a lightly floured surface to roughly a 15-inch round. Wrap loosely around the rolling pin and transfer to the prepared baking sheet. Add about ⅓ cup pesto to the center of the crust, leaving a 2- to 3-inch border. Layer tomato slices on top. Brush olive oil over tomatoes, then sprinkle with salt and freshly ground pepper. Fold edges of crust up and over, partially overlapping the filling. Pinch dough where it overlaps itself to seal in the filling and prevent leaks. Brush Egg Wash on crust and sprinkle with Parmesan. Bake for 40 to 45 minutes or until the crust is golden brown.

To serve: Place the burrata ball in the center of the warm galette. Drizzle the top with additional pesto and garnish with fresh basil. Serve immediately.

Single Butter Pie Dough
(page 33)

PESTO

¼ cup (34 g) pine nuts

2 cloves garlic

¼ teaspoon fine sea salt

¼ teaspoon freshly ground black pepper

2 cups packed fresh basil leaves

½ cup extra virgin olive oil

½ cup (35 g) freshly grated Parmesan

TO ASSEMBLE

1 pound (453 g) heirloom tomato, sliced

2 tablespoons olive oil

Fine sea salt and pepper, to taste

Egg Wash (page 275)

¼ cup (28 g) freshly shredded Parmesan

TO SERVE

8 ounces (227 g) burrata

¼ cup pesto

2 tablespoons fresh basil, chiffonade cut

Makes
1
GALETTE

SUMMER

page
155

Tomatillo, Chicken, *and* Sweet Corn Galette

Fresh sweet corn in the summer is one of the joys of living in the Midwest. My mom used to bring home bushels of corn from a local farm to add to the dinner table and to freeze to enjoy throughout the year. I wanted to capture that summer flavor along with one of my beloved Tex-Mex combinations: tangy tomatillos, chicken, cilantro, and Monterey Jack cheese. This savory galette is a summer hit, perfect for a potluck or cookout.

Single Butter Pie Dough (page 33)

SALSA VERDE

1 pound tomatillos, husked

½ med. white onion, chopped

2 cloves garlic

1 jalapeño, seeded if desired and sliced

1 teaspoon cumin

1 teaspoon fine sea salt

½ bunch fresh cilantro

2 tablespoons vegetable oil

TO ASSEMBLE

4 ears fresh sweet corn, husked (about 2½ cups corn kernels)

fine sea salt and pepper, to taste

1 egg

½ cup heavy cream

1 cup salsa verde

2 cups pulled rotisserie chicken

2 scallions, sliced

2 cups shredded Monterey Jack cheese, divided

Egg Wash (page 275)

Preheat oven to 375°F. Line a 12-inch cast-iron skillet with parchment paper.

To make the salsa verde: Fill a large pot half full with water. Add tomatillos, onion, garlic, and jalapeños. Over medium-high heat, bring to a boil. Reduce temperature to medium and simmer for 25 to 30 minutes, until onions and jalapeños are tender and tomatillos have darkened in color. Remove from heat and allow to rest for 10 minutes. Using a slotted spoon, scoop vegetables into a blender pitcher. Add ¼ cup of the cooking liquid, cumin, and salt. Cover and blend for 15 seconds. Add cilantro, stems down. The blender will pull cilantro down by the stems for even blending. Blend until the salsa is completely smooth.

Empty pot and wipe dry. Add oil and heat over medium. Add salsa to pot and bring to a simmer. Cook for 10 to 15 minutes. Allow to cool completely.

To make the filling: Fill a large pot with water and bring to a boil over medium-high heat. Add husked corn, return to a boil, and cook for 10 to 15 minutes. Remove ears from water and allow to cool until they can be handled. With a sharp knife, cut the kernels from the cob into a medium bowl. Add salt and pepper to taste.

In a medium bowl, whisk egg and cream until fully incorporated. Stir in salsa verde, chicken, scallions, 1 cup cheese, and corn kernels until combined.

To assemble galette: Roll out dough on a lightly floured surface to roughly a 15-inch round. Wrap loosely around the rolling pin and transfer to the prepared skillet. Add filling to the dough. Fold edges of crust up and over the filling. Pinch crust where it overlaps itself to seal in the filling and prevent

SUMMER

Makes

1

SKILLET GALETTE

page
156

G✳F

TO GARNISH

¼ cup chopped fresh cilantro

lime wedges

jalapeño slices

leaks. Brush Egg Wash on top crust. Bake for 30 minutes, then add remaining 1 cup cheese to the top. Bake an additional 25 to 30 minutes or until crust is golden brown and cheese is bubbling and golden.

To serve: Top the warm galette with chopped cilantro and serve with lime wedges and jalapeño slices.

❋ *Not all rotisserie chicken is gluten-free. Please check your chicken carefully if a gluten-free galette is desired.*

Homemade salsa verde is amazing, and I highly recommend you try it! You can certainly make it ahead of time and store in the freezer. However, if you just don't have time or easy access to tomatillos, 1 cup of storebought salsa verde works just fine.

Southwest Quiche

Quiche is probably one of my favorite comfort foods, and this is my go-to recipe. Shredded potatoes, sausage, and cheese are classic breakfast foods, but it's the peppers that make this feel more like dinner. Whenever you eat it, it will make a hearty meal.

Parbake crust in a deep-dish pie plate according to the instructions on page 41, then reduce oven temperature to 375°F.

In a medium skillet or nonstick pan, melt butter and add olive oil. Add shredded potatoes, salt, and pepper. Cook over medium-high heat for about 8 minutes, stirring occasionally. Potatoes will finish cooking in the oven, so no need to get them fully cooked. Mix in scallions, bell pepper, and jalapeño, and set aside. In a separate pan, brown sausage over medium heat and add to potato mixture.

In the bowl of a stand mixer fitted with the whisk attachment, beat milk and cream on medium speed for 2 minutes. Add eggs and beat for an additional 2 minutes.

Add half of the potato mixture to the parbaked crust. Layer about half of the cheese on top and then add remainder of potato mixture. Top with the rest of the cheese and pour egg mixture evenly over the filling.

Set quiche on a rimmed baking sheet and loosely cover with foil. Bake for 45 minutes, then remove foil. Bake for an additional 20 to 30 minutes or until the top is golden brown and a cake tester inserted in the middle comes out clean. Serve immediately.

Single Butter Pie Dough (page 33)

FILLING

1 tablespoon butter

1 tablespoon olive oil

1½ cups (300 g) shredded potatoes

1 teaspoon fine sea salt

½ teaspoon freshly ground black pepper

½ cup sliced scallions

1 red bell pepper, cored, seeded, and finely chopped

1 jalapeño pepper, cored, seeded, and finely chopped

½ pound (227 g) ground sausage

¾ cup whole milk

¾ cup heavy cream

4 eggs

2 cups (225 g) shredded Colby Jack cheese

Makes
1
DEEP-DISH
PIE

G✳F

SUMMER

Fall

Brown Butter Caramel Apple Pie

When humid summer days finally give way to crisp evenings and the maple leaves show signs of red and yellow, our family heads to a local orchard to pick apples. We love to fill a wagon with apples and taste them right off the tree. Even though apples are a year-round fruit, I remember them being extra special in autumn–especially the sticky caramel-covered apples of my childhood. For me this apple pie encapsulates fall with its rich amber flavors. The browned butter adds a nutty aroma, and the Salted Caramel makes for the perfect nostalgic combination of flavors.

To make the crumb: Set a medium heatproof bowl near the stove. Melt butter in a medium saucepan over medium heat. Whisk butter and continue to cook until small brown specks appear near the bottom of the pan. Butter should have a nutty aroma and take on a light brown color. Remove from heat and pour into the bowl to prevent further cooking and possibly burning butter. Cool completely. Stir remaining crumb ingredients into the cooled butter. When a crumb starts to form, work with your hands until ingredients are incorporated. Set aside.

To make the crust: Preheat oven to 375°F. Roll out dough on a lightly floured surface to a roughly 15-inch round. Wrap loosely around the rolling pin and transfer to a deep-dish pie plate. Cut off any extra crust and crimp edges.

To make the filling: Place apple slices in a medium bowl and toss with lemon juice. In a small bowl, combine sugar, cinnamon, and salt. Pour over the apples. Add ¼ cup Salted Caramel and stir until the apples are evenly coated. Pour apples into the prepared crust. Crumble crumb mixture evenly over apples.

If desired, roll out any remaining dough scraps and make cutouts to decorate the top of the pie. Bake for about 45 minutes or until the top and crust are golden brown. Serve warm with additional Salted Caramel and Vanilla Bean Ice Cream.

Single Butter Pie Dough (page 33)

BROWN BUTTER CRUMB
½ cup (113 g) unsalted butter

½ cup (90 g) brown sugar

¼ cup (50 g) granulated sugar

½ teaspoon fine sea salt

½ cup (50 g) coarsely chopped pecans

1 cup + 2 tablespoons (146 g) all-purpose flour

FILLING
6 cups (690 g) cored, peeled, and sliced apples (about 6)

1 tablespoon fresh lemon juice

⅓ cup (66 g) sugar

1 teaspoon cinnamon

¼ teaspoon fine sea salt

¼ cup Salted Caramel (page 289), plus more for serving

PAIRS WITH

Salted Caramel (page 289)

Vanilla Bean Ice Cream (page 270)

Makes
1
DEEP-DISH PIE

FALL

7 Favorite Apple
VARIETIES FOR *Pies*

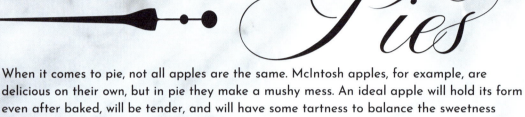

When it comes to pie, not all apples are the same. McIntosh apples, for example, are delicious on their own, but in pie they make a mushy mess. An ideal apple will hold its form even after baked, will be tender, and will have some tartness to balance the sweetness of the pie. I tested these seven apple varieties in pies, and this is what I found. Select the variety with your preferred tartness and firmness to make the pie that best fits your taste.

1

Jonagold
This apple won the most votes when I held a family apple pie taste test. They are a cross between Golden Delicious and Jonathan apples. They retain more crispness than Golden Delicious and have an excellent balance of tart and sweet.

2

Northern Spy
Spys for pies— Northern Spy apples are one of the best combinations of tart and sweet, are firm enough to hold their shape when baked, and are one of my top choices for pie. They can be difficult to find in grocery stores. Look for them in the fall at orchards and farmers' markets.

3

Braeburn
The flavor of Braeburn apples intensifies during baking, and they retain a lot of their juiciness without the pie becoming runny, making them an excellent choice for baking.

4

Pink Lady

One of my top choices
for pies, Pink Lady
apples are the
perfect combination
of sweet and tart and
retain their flavor and
some of their crispness
after baking.

5

Golden Delicious

With a mild sweet flavor
and just enough firmness to
hold their shape, baked Golden
Delicious apples are the softest
variety in this group.

6

Granny Smith

Granny Smiths are one of the most tart and
firm apples, making them great for pies.
They hold their shape, are still slightly crisp
after baking, and have a tart flavor that
complements the sweetness in the pie.

7

Honeycrisp

True to its name, this apple is the most
crisp in my test group, yielding firm
apple pieces in the finished pie. The
flavor is mild and more sweet than tart.

Fried Apple Hand Pies

Somewhere between an apple fritter and an apple pie, these little hand pies are warm comfort and perfect for a cool autumn day. Try them with hot apple cider or coffee, served with a side of warm Salted Caramel for dipping.

Double Butter Pie Dough
(page 33)

4 cups (460 g) peeled, cored, and diced apples (about 4)

¼ cup (45 g) brown sugar

1½ teaspoons cinnamon

1 teaspoon vanilla bean paste

¼ cup (56 g) unsalted butter

neutral oil for frying

½ cup (100 g) sugar

1 tablespoon cinnamon

❋ *These pies taste best fresh. You can freeze unfried pies. Allow frozen pies to thaw in the refrigerator for 4 hours before frying.*

In a medium bowl, combine apples, brown sugar, cinnamon, and vanilla bean paste. Stir until the apples are coated. In a skillet over medium-high heat, melt butter. Add apple mixture and cook for 5 to 7 minutes or until apples are tender but not soft.

Line a baking sheet with parchment paper. On a lightly floured surface, roll out half of the dough to ⅛-inch thick. Use a 4-inch round cookie cutter to make 10 cutouts, rerolling the dough as necessary. Place 2 tablespoons filling near the center of each dough round. Brush the edges with water, fold the dough into a half-circle, and press to seal. Crimp the edges with a fork. Set each hand pie on the lined baking sheet and continue forming pies with the remaining half of the dough and filling. Refrigerate pies for 30 minutes before frying.

Clip a candy thermometer to a heavy-bottomed pot or Dutch oven, pour in 3 to 4 inches oil, and preheat oil to 350°F. Line a rimmed baking sheet with paper towels and set a cooling rack on top. In a medium bowl, combine sugar and cinnamon. Using a metal skimmer, carefully lower 2 or 3 pies into the preheated oil, 1 at a time. Fry until golden brown, about 3 minutes per side. Remove with the metal skimmer and place on the prepared cooling rack to drain. After about 1 minute of draining, place each pie in the cinnamon sugar mixture, gently turning to coat both sides. Return to the rack to cool for a few more minutes. Serve warm with Salted Caramel.

If you want to avoid frying, you can bake these hand pies instead. Preheat your oven to 375°F and line a baking sheet with a silicon baking mat or parchment paper. Place formed, chilled pies on the baking sheet, leaving at least 1 inch of space between pies. Cut three small vents in the top of each pie. Bake for 25 to 30 minutes or until the outside is golden and the filling is bubbling. Melt ¼ cup salted butter. Brush pies with butter and sprinkle with the cinnamon sugar mixture. Serve warm.

FALL

Makes about
20

PAIRS WITH

Salted Caramel
(page 289)

Caramel Apple Spice Galette

As the maple leaves turn to reds and yellows, the school buses return to the neighborhood, and crisp breezes bring out cardigans, the warm spices of fall begin to appear in coffee shops and bakeries. This easy to pull together galette is the perfect complement to all of fall's cozy charms. It's delicious all on its own but even better with Salted Caramel and Toffee Pecans–and ice cream.

Preheat oven to 375°F. Line a half-sheet pan with parchment paper or a silicone baking mat. Roll out pie dough to about a 15-inch round. Wrap loosely around the rolling pin and transfer to the prepared baking sheet.

Add apple slices to a medium bowl. Add lemon juice and toss to coat. In a small bowl, mix together sugar, cinnamon, nutmeg, allspice, and cardamom. Sprinkle mixture over apples and stir until evenly coated.

With an offset spatula, spread Salted Caramel in a thin layer in the center of the crust, leaving a 2- to 3-inch border. Top caramel with apples. Fold edges of crust up and over, partially overlapping the filling. Pinch crust where it overlaps to seal in the filling and prevent leaks. Brush Egg Wash on top crust and sprinkle with turbinado sugar. Bake for 40 to 45 minutes or until the filling is bubbling and the top crust is golden brown. Allow to cool 15 minutes and serve warm with more Salted Caramel and Toffee Pecans.

❋ To revive, place cold galette slices on a baking sheet in a 300°F oven for 10 minutes.

Single Maple Pie Dough (page 34)

FILLING

4 cups (460 g) peeled, cored, and sliced apples (about 4)

2 tablespoons fresh lemon juice

2 tablespoons sugar

2 teaspoons cinnamon

¼ teaspoon nutmeg

¼ teaspoon allspice

¼ teaspoon cardamom

½ cup Salted Caramel (page 289), plus more for serving

Egg Wash (page 275)

2 tablespoons turbinado sugar

PAIRS WITH

Salted Caramel (page 289)

Toffee Pecans (page 290)

Makes **1** GALETTE

FALL

page **169**

Cinnamon Roll Blueberry Apple Pie

Pie dough made into little cinnamon rolls creates a cute top for this blueberry and apple pie that is so good any time of the day, even for breakfast. Drizzled with a cream cheese glaze, it's almost like a fruit-filled Danish pastry. It's a fun, sweet pie, and a great addition to any apple pie lineup.

CRUST

Double Butter Pie Dough (page 33)

⅔ cup (132 g) brown sugar

2 teaspoons cinnamon

FILLING

4 cups (460 grams) cored, peeled, and sliced apples (about 4)

1 cup (180 g) blueberries

2 tablespoons fresh lemon juice

¼ cup (56 g) unsalted butter, melted

½ cup (90 g) light brown sugar

1 egg, room temperature

1 tablespoon vanilla bean paste

½ cup (65 g) all-purpose flour

1½ tablespoons cinnamon

½ teaspoon fine sea salt

Egg Wash (page 275)

CREAM CHEESE GLAZE

2 ounces (57 g) cream cheese, softened

2 tablespoons half and half

1 teaspoon vanilla extract

1¼ cups (138 g) confectioners' sugar

Preheat oven to 375°F.

To make the crust: Roll out the first dough disk on a lightly floured surface to roughly a 15-inch round. Wrap loosely around the rolling pin and transfer to a deep-dish pie plate. Trim extra crust and crimp edges. Loosely cover with plastic wrap and refrigerate until needed. In a small bowl, combine cinnamon and sugar. Roll out the second dough disk to roughly a 15-inch square. Evenly cover the surface of the dough with cinnamon sugar and roll the rolling pin over the sugar to help it stick to the dough. Roll dough into a log, cover with plastic wrap, and refrigerate for at least 30 minutes.

To make the filling: Add apple slices and blueberries to a medium bowl and toss with lemon juice to coat. In the bowl of a stand mixer fitted with the paddle attachment, add melted butter, brown sugar, egg, vanilla bean paste, flour, cinnamon, and salt. Beat on medium speed until all ingredients are fully incorporated. Scrape the sides and bottom of the bowl to ensure even mixing. Pour mixture over fruit and stir until fruit is evenly coated. Pour into the prepared pie crust and level filling so it is as flat as possible.

Remove dough log from the refrigerator and cut into ¼-inch slices. Place slices on top of the pie filling. Place slices tightly together to fully cover the top of the pie. Brush with Egg Wash.

Bake for 50 to 60 minutes or until the top of the pie is golden brown and the filling is bubbling. Whisk together cream cheese glaze ingredients and drizzle on pie before serving, or serve the glaze on the side so guests can add their desired amount.

✽ *To revive, place cold pie slices on a baking sheet and warm in a 300°F oven for about 12 minutes.*

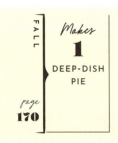

FALL

Makes
1
DEEP-DISH
PIE

Speculoos Apple Cream Cheese Pie

We love speculoos cookies and cookie butter at our house, especially the Biscoff variety. They are a fabulous addition to an apple pie, with all their delicious spices and crispness. This pie uses speculoos cookies for the crust and combines a cream cheese filling with apples and cookie butter for a cookie-licious, cheesecake-like apple pie. Topped with Cream Cheese Whipped Cream, this one makes a beautiful presentation and is a lovely twist on the beloved apple pie.

Preheat oven to 350°F. Press crust into a deep-dish pie plate and set aside.

To make the filling: In the bowl of a stand mixer fitted with the paddle attachment, beat cream cheese, sugar, and vanilla extract on medium speed until fluffy, about 3 minutes. Add eggs, cookie butter, and buttermilk, and beat on medium speed until fully incorporated and batter is smooth. Scrape the bottom and sides of the bowl to ensure even mixing. Remove bowl from stand mixer.

Peel and core apples. Cut each into 8 wedges and slice each wedge in half. You should have about 2 cups. Add apples to batter and stir to combine with a rubber spatula. Pour batter into prepared crust.

To make the crumb: In a medium bowl, whisk together all the dry ingredients until spices are evenly distributed. Pour melted butter and vanilla bean paste over dry ingredients and mix with a rubber spatula or your hands until a crumb forms. Crumble chunks of crumb on top of apple batter.

Bake for about 45 minutes, or until the center is only slightly jiggly and a cake tester inserted in the edge comes out clean. Allow to cool completely.

Add the Cream Cheese Whipped Cream to a pastry bag fitted with a large star tip. Pipe onto the cooled pie. Drizzle with Salted Caramel and garnish with cookies, if desired. Serve immediately or store in the refrigerator until ready to serve.

Deep-Dish Speculoos Crumb Crust (variation; page 52)

FILLING

8 ounces (227 g) cream cheese, softened

½ cup (100 g) sugar

1 teaspoon vanilla extract

2 eggs, room temperature

½ cup (145 g) cookie butter

¼ cup buttermilk

2 apples (about 230 g)

CRUMB

1 cup (130 g) all-purpose flour

⅓ cup (26 g) old-fashioned oatmeal

⅔ cup (119 g) brown sugar

⅓ cup (35 g) chopped pecans

1 teaspoon cinnamon

⅛ teaspoon nutmeg

⅛ teaspoon ground cloves

⅛ teaspoon allspice

(continued)

PAIRS WITH

Cream Cheese Whipped Cream (page 277)

Salted Caramel (page 289)

Makes

1

DEEP-DISH PIE

FALL

⅛ teaspoon ginger

¼ teaspoon fine sea salt

½ cup (113 g) unsalted butter, melted

1 teaspoon vanilla bean paste

TO GARNISH
Cream Cheese Whipped Cream (page 277)

Salted Caramel, optional (page 289)

5 speculoos cookies (such as Biscoff), optional

Chocolate Hazelnut Baklava Pie

Baklava can be a little labor intensive, but if you set up a station and sit down to assemble this many-layered pie, it can be a relaxing and enjoyable dessert to make. Baklava is a winner at gatherings–it is so beloved and savored by guests. This version, which takes the ancient flavors and adds chocolate hazelnut spread, is also amazing. I got the idea at a Greek bakery in Manhattan that makes so many varieties of baklava it's impossible to choose. Their chocolate and hazelnut was incredible, and I wanted to re-create that treat in the form of this pie.

Preheat oven to 350°F.

Finely chop the nuts in the bowl of a food processor. Add chocolate chips, sugar, cinnamon, and cloves. Pulse to combine.

In a medium heatproof bowl, add chocolate hazelnut spread and coconut oil. Place in the microwave at 30% power for 45 seconds. Take out and stir. Continue microwaving at 30% power in 30-second intervals until the mixture is thin and smooth.

Line the bottom of a 10-inch springform pan with a parchment round. Brush the parchment paper and sides of the pan with butter. Unroll phyllo dough. Trim dough to the size of your pan. Phyllo dough dries out quickly, so keep it covered with a layer of plastic wrap topped with a damp towel. Place 2 sheets of phyllo dough in the pan. Brush the top of dough layer 1 with melted butter and top with 2 to 3 tablespoons nut mixture. Add two more sheets of phyllo. Brush dough layer 2 with chocolate mixture and then top with 2 to 3 tablespoons nut mixture. Repeat these steps, alternating between butter and chocolate with nuts, until you run out of nut mixture. For the top layer, add 2 sheets of phyllo, brush with butter, then add 2 more sheets and brush with more butter. With a sharp knife, cut baklava into a pattern of diamonds or pie wedges. Make sure to cut all the way to the bottom of the pan. If you have any remaining butter, drizzle it over the top of the dough. Place pan on a rimmed baking sheet to catch any drips and bake for 35 to 40 minutes or until golden brown on top.

(continued)

BAKLAVA

1 cup (130 g) hazelnuts

1 cup (120 g) shelled pistachios

¼ cup mini semisweet chocolate chips

¼ cup (50 g) sugar

1 teaspoon ground cinnamon

¼ teaspoon ground cloves

½ cup (113 g) salted butter, melted

1 cup (280 g) chocolate hazelnut spread (such as Nutella)

1 tablespoon coconut oil

1 pound phyllo dough, thawed

SYRUP

½ cup water

½ cup (100 g) sugar

peel of ½ lemon, without pith

1 teaspoon vanilla extract

½ cup (170 g) honey

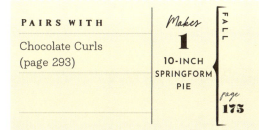

PAIRS WITH

Chocolate Curls
(page 293)

Makes
1
10-INCH
SPRINGFORM
PIE

FALL

TO GARNISH

2 tablespoons finely chopped pistachios

2 tablespoons finely chopped hazelnuts

Chocolate Curls (page 293)

While baking, make the syrup. In a saucepan over medium-high heat, bring water, sugar, lemon peel, and vanilla extract to a boil. Reduce heat to medium. Add honey and continue cooking until mixture bubbles and liquid is a clear amber. You may have to move aside the foamy top to see if liquid is no longer cloudy. Strain syrup through a fine mesh sieve.

After removing baklava from the oven, immediately spoon syrup evenly over the top. The syrup will sizzle. Allow to cool completely, then cover and allow to rest at least 2 hours in the refrigerator before unmolding. Place on a rimmed serving plate and remove the sides of the springform pan. Garnish with pistachios, hazelnuts, and Chocolate Curls.

TIPS FOR MELTING CHOCOLATE

Chocolate can be melted in a double boiler on the stove or a heatproof bowl in the microwave. The key to success is to melt on low heat, slowly. Follow these tips to achieve smooth, easy to work with melted chocolate.

* Take care not to overheat chocolate. It burns easily and cannot be salvaged once burned. When using the microwave, use a low power setting and short times to ensure chocolate is not overheated.

* Avoid water when melting chocolate. Even a drop of water can make chocolate seize, rendering it unusable.

* For best results, use high-quality chocolate bars, chopped, or chocolate feves or wafers designed for melting.

* If your chocolate is too thick, you can thin it with a small amount of coconut oil or vegetable shortening. Avoid butter, which can make chocolate seize.

Caramel Pear Pie

Apple is my usual go-to fall pie, but pears also go amazingly with fall spices, and this is a great way to mix things up with your fall baking.

Double Butter Pie Dough (see page 33)

FILLING

6 cups (700 grams) cored, peeled, and sliced pears

1 tablespoon fresh lemon juice

⅓ cup (59 g) brown sugar

1 tablespoon cornstarch

1 teaspoon cinnamon

½ teaspoon nutmeg

¼ teaspoon fine sea salt

½ cup Salted Caramel (page 289), plus more for serving

Egg Wash (page 275)

3 tablespoons turbinado sugar

Preheat oven to 375°F. Roll out first disk of dough on a lightly floured surface to roughly a 15-inch round. Wrap loosely around the rolling pin and transfer to a deep-dish pie plate. Cut off any extra crust and crimp edges.

To make the filling: Place pear slices in a medium bowl and toss with lemon juice to coat. In a small bowl, combine brown sugar, cornstarch, cinnamon, nutmeg, and salt. Pour over the pears. Add Salted Caramel and stir until the pears are evenly coated. Pour into the prepared crust.

Roll out the second half of the dough on a lightly floured surface. Wrap loosely around the rolling pin and place on top of the pie. Cut off any excess dough, connect to the bottom crust, and crimp the edge. With a sharp knife, cut vents in the top crust. Brush with Egg Wash and sprinkle with turbinado sugar. (For decorative top crust ideas, see page 44.)

Bake for about 45 to 50 minutes or until the top crust is golden brown. Serve warm with more Salted Caramel, Vanilla Bean Ice Cream, and Toffee Pecans.

FALL

Makes
1
DEEP-DISH PIE

page **178**

PAIRS WITH

Vanilla Bean Ice Cream (page 279)

Toffee Pecans (page 290)

White Chocolate Macadamia Nut Tart

I've always loved white chocolate with macadamia nuts. This salty sweet tart is chewy in the center and richly buttery. The white chocolate ganache with Chocolate Curls makes a beautiful presentation and will look great in any fall spread.

Preheat oven to 350°F. Press dough into a 10-inch tart pan. Generously dock the crust and parbake for 10 minutes.

To make the filling: In the bowl of a stand mixer fitted with the paddle attachment, beat butter and brown sugar on medium speed until light and fluffy, about 3 minutes. Add eggs and vanilla and beat until fully incorporated. In a small bowl, whisk together flour and salt. Add to butter mixture and mix just until combined. Scrape sides and bottom of bowl to ensure even mixing. Remove bowl from the stand mixer and stir in macadamia nuts with a rubber spatula. Add to the parbaked crust. Bake for 20 to 25 minutes or until the crust and top are golden brown. Allow to cool completely.

To make the ganache: Add chopped chocolate to a heatproof bowl. Heat the heavy cream in a small saucepan over medium-high heat until steaming but not boiling. Remove from heat, then pour cream over chocolate and allow to sit for about 1 minute. Using a rubber spatula, stir until chocolate is totally melted and combined. Allow ganache to sit for 5 to 10 minutes, until it thickens a little, then pour over cooled tart. Cover and refrigerate for 1 hour or until ganache sets before removing the sides of the pan. Keep in the refrigerator until ready to serve. Garnish with White Chocolate Curls, Caramel Shards, and more macadamia nuts.

Press-In Shortbread Tart Dough (page 49)

FILLING

3 tablespoons unsalted butter, softened

¾ cup (135 g) light brown sugar

2 eggs, room temperature

1 tablespoon vanilla extract

¼ cup (33 g) all-purpose flour

½ teaspoon fine sea salt

¾ cup (100 g) chopped macadamia nuts, plus more to garnish

GANACHE TOPPING

4 ounces (113 g) white chocolate, chopped

½ cup heavy cream

TO GARNISH
White Chocolate Curls (page 293)

PAIRS WITH

Caramel Shards
(page 291)

White Chocolate Curls
(page 293)

Makes
1
10-INCH
TART

FALL

Caramel Brownie Skillet Pie

Chocolate and caramel have long been a top choice on a dessert spread. This skillet pie tastes best when it's still warm from the oven and the brownie and Salted Caramel are soft, gooey deliciousness. Don't worry about getting a tidy piece with this pie. Just scoop it up and top with ice cream for an insanely delicious dessert win.

1½ Butter Pie Dough (page 33)

1 cup (225 g) unsalted butter, melted and cooled

¾ cup (135 g) brown sugar

¾ cup (150 g) sugar

4 eggs, room temperature

1 tablespoon vanilla extract

4 ounces (113 g) bittersweet chocolate, melted and cooled

½ cup (46 g) unsweetened cocoa powder

½ cup (65 g) all-purpose flour

½ teaspoon fine sea salt

1 cup Salted Caramel (page 289), plus more for serving

Preheat oven to 425°F. Roll out dough on a lightly floured surface to roughly a 17-inch round. Wrap loosely around the rolling pin and transfer to a 12-inch cast-iron skillet. Tuck any extra crust under to create an even edge. Parbake per instructions on page 41. Reduce oven temperature to 350°F.

To make the brownie filling: In the bowl of a stand mixer fitted with the whisk attachment, beat melted butter and sugars until combined. Add eggs one at a time, mixing between each addition. Add vanilla and melted chocolate and mix just until combined. Remove bowl from the stand mixer. In a medium bowl, sift cocoa. Add flour and salt and whisk to combine. Add to the butter mixture and stir by hand with a rubber spatula just until combined. Pour into the parbaked crust. Dollop Salted Caramel on top and swirl into the batter.

Bake for 25 to 30 minutes or until the edges have set and the center is slightly jiggly. Allow to cool at least 30 minutes before cutting. Serve with Vanilla Bean Ice Cream and more Salted Caramel.

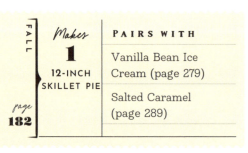

FALL

Makes
1
12-INCH
SKILLET PIE

PAIRS WITH

Vanilla Bean Ice Cream (page 279)

Salted Caramel (page 289)

Frangipane Plum Tart

Frangipane is a sweet, creamy almond filling that pairs nicely with fruit. This tart is an autumn treasure with fresh purple-red plums baked on top of the delicious filling. My colleague Maya, who often bakes beautiful, creative desserts, inspired the rose shape for this tart. The colors, aromas, and flavors are so reminiscent of the season and make a pretty addition to a Thanksgiving pie spread.

To make the crust: Preheat oven to 350°F. Press tart dough into a 10-inch tart pan. Generously dock with a fork and parbake for 10 minutes. While still hot, use a tamper or the back of a spoon to lightly press down the center of the crust, leaving a ¾-inch edge.

To make the frangipane: In the bowl of a stand mixer fitted with the paddle attachment, beat butter, sugar, egg, and almond and vanilla extracts until smooth. Whisk salt into almond flour and add to the butter mixture. Beat until smooth. Pour into parbaked crust.

To assemble: In a medium bowl, whisk together sugar, cornstarch, and cinnamon. In a separate bowl, combine sliced plums and lemon juice, tossing to coat. Add sugar mixture and stir until plums are evenly coated. To create a rosette top, start on the outer edge of the tart and arrange the plums skin-side up, one ring at a time. Offset each new ring so the plums don't line up, creating a more natural floral shape. Sprinkle the top with the turbinado sugar and bake for 40 to 45 minutes or until the filling has set. Let tart cool at least ten minutes before removing the sides of the pan. Serve warm with Vanilla Bean Ice Cream.

✻ *I like to use black plums, but you can use your favorite variety.*

Press-In Shortbread Tart Dough (page 49)

FRANGIPANE
⅓ cup (74 g) unsalted butter, softened

⅓ cup (66 g) sugar

1 egg, room temperature

½ teaspoon almond extract

1 teaspoon vanilla extract

¼ teaspoon fine sea salt

⅔ cup (63 g) almond flour

PLUMS
2 tablespoons (25 g) sugar

2 teaspoons cornstarch

½ teaspoon cinnamon

3½ cups (500 g) pitted and thinly sliced fresh plums

1 tablespoon fresh lemon juice

2 tablespoons turbinado sugar

PAIRS WITH

Vanilla Bean Ice Cream (page 279)

Makes **1** 10-INCH TART

FALL

page **185**

G✻F

Crème Brûlée Tart

Crème brûlée has been around for centuries in a variety of forms throughout Europe. The name is French and translates to "burned cream"–the base is a rich custard topped with sugar that is caramelized into a golden, slightly burned, and candy-hard layer. This tart makes a great dessert for a dinner party or gathering on a cool fall evening.

Press-In Shortbread Tart Dough (page 49)

3 egg yolks

1 tablespoon cornstarch

⅔ cup (133 g) sugar, divided

1 vanilla bean

1 cup heavy cream

¼ teaspoon fine sea salt

TO SERVE

3 tablespoons sugar

To make the crust: Preheat oven to 350°F. Press tart dough into a 10-inch tart pan. Generously dock with a fork and parbake for 15 minutes. While still hot, use a tamper or the back of a spoon to lightly press down the center of the crust, leaving a ¾-inch edge. Reduce oven temperature to 325°F.

To make the filling: In the bowl of a stand mixer fitted with the whisk attachment, mix egg yolks, cornstarch, and ½ cup sugar on low. Using a sharp knife, cut vanilla bean lengthwise on a cutting board. Open the bean and scrape out seeds and add to the yolk mixture.

In a medium saucepan, add heavy cream, salt, and remaining ¼ cup sugar. Whisk together and cook over medium heat until mixture reaches a simmer. With the mixer running on its lowest setting, slowly pour in the hot cream. Mix until fully combined. Pour mixture through a fine mesh sieve into a spouted bowl. Place parbaked tart crust on a baking sheet. Pour cream mixture into the crust. Bake for 35 to 40 minutes or until the edges have set and the center is still a little jiggly. Allow to cool completely, then cover and refrigerate for at least 2 hours.

When ready to serve, sprinkle the top with sugar. Using a kitchen torch, melt and caramelize the sugar until it is a deep golden brown. If you don't have a kitchen torch, you can place the tart under the broiler for about 1 to 2 minutes. Do not leave unattended, as the sugar can burn quickly. Remove sides of tart pan and serve immediately with Salted Caramel, if desired.

FALL

Makes

1

10-INCH
TART

PAIRS WITH

Salted Caramel
(page 289)

G✳F

Oatmeal Cream Pies

I grew up with the packaged version of Oatmeal Cream Pies in my school lunches and loved them as a kid. This is the grown-up version, and they are so much better–all the warm childhood flavor in freshly baked, soft, chewy oatmeal cookies with a buttercream filling. These are amazing on a crisp fall day with a cup of hot coffee.

To make the cookies: Preheat oven to 350°F. Line two baking sheets with parchment paper or silicone baking mats.

In the bowl of a stand mixer fitted with the paddle attachment, beat butter and brown sugar until light and fluffy, about 5 minutes. Add eggs, molasses, corn syrup, and vanilla bean paste. Beat until combined. In a small bowl, combine flour, oatmeal, baking soda, salt, and cinnamon. Add to the butter mixture and beat until combined.

Scoop dough with a 1-ounce cookie scoop onto the prepared baking sheets. Leave about 2 inches between each cookie. Bake each sheet for 9 to 11 minutes or until golden brown. Allow cookies to cool on the pan for about 5 minutes before transferring to a cooling rack.

To make the filling: In the bowl of a stand mixer fitted with the paddle attachment, beat butter, heavy cream, salt, vanilla, and 1 cup confectioners' sugar for 3 minutes, until fluffy. Scrape the bowl, including the bottom, to make sure all ingredients are incorporated.

Add remaining confectioners' sugar ½ cup at a time, beating well between each addition, until filling reaches a spreadable consistency. You can add a little more cream if it's too thick or a little more confectioners' sugar if it's too thin.

Scoop the buttercream into a pastry bag fitted with a large round tip. Divide cookies into pairs, matching by size. Pipe a thick layer of filling on the flat side of one cookie and top with the second cookie. Press lightly together. Serve immediately or store in an airtight container at room temperature until ready to eat.

COOKIES

1 cup unsalted butter, softened

1¼ cups (225 g) light brown sugar

2 eggs, room temperature

1 tablespoon unsulfured molasses

1 tablespoon corn syrup

1 tablespoon vanilla bean paste

2¼ cups (293 g) all-purpose flour

2 cups (160 g) old-fashioned oatmeal

1 teaspoon baking soda

½ teaspoon fine sea salt

½ teaspoon ground cinnamon

BUTTERCREAM FILLING

¾ cup (169 g) unsalted butter, softened

¼ cup heavy cream

½ teaspoon fine sea salt

2 teaspoons vanilla bean paste

2½ cups (275 g) confectioners' sugar, divided

Makes
20
PIES

FALL

Mini Pecan Tarts

Mini tarts are a perfect solution for any occasion where you need finger food, such as a gathering with lots of mingling. I've made these little two-bite pecan pies for graduation parties and showers. They're also great on a fall-themed dessert grazing board. For extra fall flair, make leaf-shaped pie crust cutouts to top some of your mini tarts.

Extra-Large Butter Pie Dough (page 33)

FILLING
2 cups (210 g) chopped pecans

½ cup (113 g) unsalted butter, melted and cooled

1 cup (180 g) brown sugar

3 tablespoons maple syrup

1 egg, room temperature

½ teaspoon fine sea salt

1 teaspoon cinnamon

1 vanilla bean

TO GARNISH
Cream Cheese Whipped Cream (page 277)

Preheat oven to 375°F. Set out two 24-well mini muffin pans. (If you only have one pan, bake the mini tarts in two batches.)

Roll out half of the dough to about ⅛-inch thick. Cut out rounds with a 3¼-inch round cookie cutter. Place one round in each well of the mini muffin pans, pressing each crust into its well with a tamper or by hand. Add about 2 teaspoons of chopped pecans to each tart crust.

In the bowl of a stand mixer fitted with the whisk attachment, mix butter, brown sugar, and maple syrup until combined. Add egg, salt, and cinnamon and mix on medium speed until fully combined. With a sharp knife on a cutting board, cut vanilla bean lengthwise. Open the bean and scrape the seeds from the inside, using the sharp edge of the knife. Add seeds to the butter mixture. Mix just until the seeds are distributed. Add about 2 to 3 teaspoons mixture to each crust. Refrigerate each pan of mini tarts for 15 minutes before baking.

Bake for about 15 to 17 minutes or until crusts are golden brown. Serve warm or cool and store in an airtight container until ready to serve. If using Cream Cheese Whipped Cream, use a pastry bag with a large star tip to pipe on the top of each mini tart just before serving.

FALL

Makes
48

GF

PAIRS WITH

Cream Cheese Whipped Cream (page 277)

Chocolate Chip Cookie Tart

This tart is like a giant chocolate chip cookie filled with gooey chocolate and topped with toasted Swiss meringue. There is so much to love in this decadent crowd-pleaser, and it makes a beautiful dessert to bring to a dinner party or gathering.

Preheat oven to 350°F. In the bowl of a stand mixer fitted with the paddle attachment, beat butter and sugar on medium speed until light and fluffy, about 3 minutes. Add egg and vanilla and beat until combined.

In a small bowl, combine flour and salt. Add to the butter mixture and mix on low just until combined. Scrape the sides and bottom of the bowl to ensure even mixing. Add chocolate chips and walnuts if using. Beat just until combined.

Press dough into a 10-inch tart pan, pressing dough up the sides of the pan. The dough will mostly fill the pan to create a large cookie with only a small indent in the center. Bake for 22 to 25 minutes until the top is golden and looks dry. The edges should be set and the center still a little jiggly. Immediately after removing from the oven, lightly tamp down the center of the crust, leaving the edges at their full height. Allow to cool for 15 minutes. Pour Chocolate Fudge Sauce into the cookie crust and cool in the refrigerator for half an hour.

To make the Swiss meringue: Whisk together egg whites and sugar in the top pan of a double boiler until completely incorporated. Cook, whisking continuously, until mixture reaches 170°F, about 5 to 6 minutes. Pour into the bowl of a stand mixer fitted with the whisk attachment. Add cream of tartar. Beat on high for about 2 minutes. Add vanilla bean paste and continue to beat on high until stiff peaks form. Scoop or pipe onto cookie tart. Toast meringue with a kitchen torch or under the oven broiler. Keep a close watch on meringue while toasting to avoid burning. Remove tart from the pan. Serve immediately with Salted Caramel or store in the refrigerator until ready to eat.

COOKIE CRUST

¾ cup (169 g) unsalted butter, softened

1 cup (180 g) brown sugar

1 egg, room temperature

1 teaspoon vanilla extract

2 cups (260 g) all-purpose flour

½ teaspoon fine sea salt

2 cups (340 g) semisweet chocolate chips

½ cup (60 g) coarsely chopped walnuts, optional

FILLING

¾ cup Chocolate Fudge Sauce (page 288)

SWISS MERINGUE

4 egg whites

1 cup (200 g) sugar

½ teaspoon cream of tartar

1 teaspoon vanilla bean paste

PAIRS WITH

Salted Caramel (page 289)

Makes
1
10-INCH
TART

FALL

Brown Sugar Maple Hand Pies

Certainly this is one of the best toaster pastry flavors of my youth, made so much better with buttery, flaky homemade pie crust and real maple icing. These intensely sweet hand pies are a fall joy, and they never last long at our house.

Double Maple Pie Dough (page 34)

FILLING
1 tablespoon unsalted butter, melted

¾ cup (135 g) brown sugar

2 tablespoons all-purpose flour

2 teaspoons vanilla extract

1 teaspoon cinnamon

Egg Wash (page 275)

ICING
¼ cup maple syrup

1 teaspoon vanilla bean paste

1½ cups (165 g) confectioners' sugar

½ cup Toffee Pecans (page 290), optional

Preheat oven to 375°F and line two baking sheets with parchment paper or silicone baking mats and set aside.

On a lightly floured surface, roll out the first disk of pie dough to about ⅛-inch thick. With a sharp knife, cut out 4½ × 3¼-inch rectangles. Cut as many rectangles as you can, and then gather the scraps and roll out dough two more times to get as many rectangles as possible. Repeat with the second disk of dough. You should have 22 rectangles total.

To make the filling: In the bowl of a stand mixer fitted with the paddle attachment, add all of the filling ingredients and mix on high for about 2 minutes, until all ingredients are fully incorporated.

Place the first two dough rectangles on the prepared baking sheet. Brush borders of both rectangles with Egg Wash. Add 1½ tablespoons brown sugar mixture to the center of one rectangle and spread a bit, leaving a ½-inch border. Place the second dough rectangle over the filling Egg Wash-side down. With the tines of a fork, crimp edges of pastry and gently poke a few holes in the top crust. Repeat with remaining dough rectangles, spacing them out over both baking sheets. Brush tops with Egg Wash. Bake one sheet at a time, storing the second sheet in the refrigerator, for 20 to 22 minutes or until golden brown on top. Transfer to a cooling rack and allow to cool completely.

To make the icing: In a medium bowl, whisk together all icing ingredients until fully incorporated. With an offset spatula, spread onto tops of cooled pastries. Top with Toffee Pecans, if using, and serve immediately. Store leftovers in an airtight container for up to 3 days or freeze for up to 2 months.

FALL

Makes
11

PAIRS WITH

Toffee Pecans
(page 290)

Peanut Butter Silk Pie

I have been making this pie for years, and it's earned a spot as one of my most popular desserts with family and friends. It's based on several different recipes; I've changed it up over the years, and this is the recipe that, to me, is perfect. It is creamy and fluffy, yet somehow still dense and peanut buttery, with a chocolatey richness from the ganache. I promise this one will not last long at any gathering. It's a perfect addition to a Thanksgiving spread–there are always a few guests who will go for peanut butter and chocolate over pumpkin.

Preheat oven to 350°F. Press crust into a deep-dish pie plate and bake for 6 minutes. Allow to cool.

In the bowl of a stand mixer fitted with the paddle attachment, beat cream cheese, peanut butter, and confectioners' sugar on medium speed until fully combined, about 2 minutes. Melt chocolate in a heatproof bowl in the microwave on low, stirring often to avoid burning. Allow chocolate to cool and then add to peanut butter mixture. Add sweetened condensed milk and vanilla and beat on medium speed for 2 minutes. Stop to scrape the sides and bottom of the bowl to ensure even mixing. Set aside.

In the bowl of a stand mixer fitted with the whisk attachment, beat cream until stiff peaks form. Add whipped cream to the peanut butter mixture and carefully fold together with a rubber spatula. Mix just until combined, taking care not to deflate the whipped cream. Pour into the prepared crust.

To make the ganache: Add chopped chocolate to a heatproof bowl. In a small saucepan, cook cream over medium-high heat until steaming but not boiling. Remove from heat and pour over chocolate. Allow to sit for about 1 minute and then stir until chocolate is completely melted and incorporated. Allow ganache to sit for 5 to 10 minutes, until it thickens a little, then pour over the top of the pie. Cover and refrigerate for at least 3 hours before serving with Whipped Cream, if desired.

Deep-Dish Chocolate Wafer Crumb Crust (page 52)

FILLING

8 ounces (227 g) cold cream cheese

1 cup (256 g) peanut butter

1 cup (110 g) confectioners' sugar

6 ounces (170 g) dark chocolate, chopped

1 (14 ounce) can sweetened condensed milk

1 teaspoon vanilla extract

1 cup heavy cream

GANACHE

3 ounces (85 g) semisweet chocolate, chopped

½ cup heavy cream

PAIRS WITH

Whipped Cream
(page 276)

Makes
1
DEEP-DISH
PIE

F
A
L
L

page
197

Chocolate Pecan Galette

Pecan lovers will adore this galette, which has all the sweetness of pecan pie balanced with the bitterness of dark chocolate. Serve warm with fresh Whipped Cream while the chocolate is still gooey or cut slices from the cooled galette for a handheld snack. This rustic galette comes together quickly and will be a top pick.

Single Butter Pie Dough
(page 33)

5 tablespoons (70 g) unsalted butter

½ cup (90 g) brown sugar

3 tablespoons maple syrup

½ teaspoon fine sea salt

½ teaspoon cinnamon

1 vanilla bean

6 ounces (170 g) dark chocolate, coarsely chopped

1¾ cups (175 g) pecan halves

Egg Wash (page 275)

2 tablespoons turbinado sugar

Preheat oven to 375°F. Line a half-sheet pan with parchment paper or a silicone baking mat.

In a medium heatproof bowl, melt butter. Whisk in brown sugar, maple syrup, salt, and cinnamon. With a sharp knife on a cutting board, cut vanilla bean lengthwise. Open the bean and scrape the seeds from the inside using the sharp edge of the knife. Add seeds to the butter mixture. Whisk until seeds are evenly distributed. Set aside.

Roll out pie dough to about a 15-inch round. Wrap loosely around the rolling pin and transfer to the prepared baking sheet. Sprinkle chopped chocolate evenly across the crust, leaving a 2- to 3-inch border. Drizzle butter mixture over chocolate, and spread pecans in a single layer on top. Fold edges of crust up and over, partially overlapping the filling. Brush Egg Wash on top crust and sprinkle with turbinado sugar. Bake for 30 to 35 minutes or until the filling is bubbling and the top crust is golden brown. Allow to cool for 15 minutes and serve warm with Whipped Cream.

❉ *If any filling leaks out of the galette while baking, it will burn on the baking sheet. Use a sharp knife to disconnect the leaked filling from the galette while it is still warm.*

FALL

Makes
1
GALETTE

PAIRS WITH

Whipped Cream
(page 276)

page
198

Kathy's Pumpkin Pie

Thanksgiving wouldn't be complete without a pumpkin pie on the dessert spread. My lifelong friend Kathy makes her own pumpkin purée, taking advantage of the fall harvest when pumpkins are plentiful. She uses the purée in her pumpkin pie recipe, which her family enjoys every Thanksgiving. Serve with plenty of Whipped Cream.

Preheat oven to 400°F. Roll out dough on a lightly floured surface to roughly a 13-inch round. Wrap loosely around the rolling pin and transfer to a 9-inch pie plate. Cut off any extra crust and crimp edges.

In a medium bowl, whisk together flour, cinnamon, nutmeg, cloves, allspice, and salt. In the bowl of a stand mixer fitted with the paddle attachment, mix pumpkin, butter, and sugars until smooth. Add spice mixture and evaporated milk. Beat on medium speed until fully combined. Scrape the sides and bottom of the bowl with a rubber spatula to ensure even mixing. Remove the bowl from the mixer.

Switch to the whisk attachment and beat whole eggs in a separate bowl until foamy, about 3 minutes. Add to the pumpkin mixture and fold in by hand with a rubber spatula. Wash bowl and whisk attachment and beat egg whites on high until stiff peaks form. Add to the pumpkin mixture and fold in by hand with a rubber spatula. Pour into prepared crust.

Bake for 10 minutes. Reduce oven temperature to 350°F and bake for 50 to 60 additional minutes or until edges are set and center jiggles slightly. Allow to cool. Serve with a generous dollop of Whipped Cream.

Single Butter Pie Dough
(page 33)

FILLING

2 tablespoons all-purpose flour

½ teaspoon cinnamon

½ teaspoon nutmeg

¼ teaspoon ground cloves

¼ teaspoon allspice

⅛ teaspoon fine sea salt

1½ cups canned or fresh pumpkin purée

1 tablespoon unsalted butter, melted

¾ cup (150 g) sugar

¾ cup (135 g) brown sugar

1 cup evaporated milk

3 eggs

2 egg whites

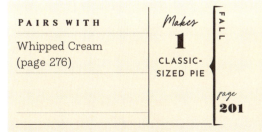

PAIRS WITH

Whipped Cream
(page 276)

Makes
1
CLASSIC-
SIZED PIE

FALL

How to MAKE FRESH Pumpkin PURÉE

My friend Kathy makes her own pumpkin purée and never uses storebought. This transforms a pumpkin pie so much that her daughters now refuse to eat anything but this fresh variety. The texture, color, and flavor are all different! You can even freeze your own purée to use throughout the year.

The type of pumpkin you use matters. The first time Kathy tried to make her own purée, she used a jack-o'-lantern style pumpkin and the results came out stringy. Be sure to use a pie pumpkin, usually located in the produce section.

1 medium pie pumpkin

Preheat oven to 400°F. Lay pumpkin on its side on a cutting board and remove the top and stem with a sharp knife. Turn upside down and cut in half. Scoop out the seeds and stringy pumpkin innards and discard. Place pumpkin halves cut-side down on a half-sheet baking pan. Roast until fork tender, about 35 to 40 minutes. Allow to cool until you can handle the pumpkin, then scoop out the pumpkin flesh with a large spoon and transfer to a food processor. Process until completely smooth. Use your purée immediately or freeze.

Makes 1½ TO **2** CUPS PUMPKIN PURÉE.

Pumpkin Cheesecake Pie

If you're like me, you might not be 100 percent all-in on pumpkin pie, but you still love the tradition of the ultimate Thanksgiving classic. If so, give this version a try with all of the autumn-spice favorites and pumpkin swirled into a cheesecake filling. This pie is my new turkey-day favorite.

Deep-Dish Graham Cracker Crumb Crust (page 52)

CHEESECAKE FILLING

16 ounces (454 g) cream cheese, softened

2 tablespoons unsalted butter, softened

⅔ cup (133 g) sugar

2 eggs

¼ cup buttermilk

2 tablespoons all-purpose flour

2 teaspoons vanilla extract

PUMPKIN CHEESECAKE FILLING

½ cup pumpkin purée

1 teaspoon cinnamon

¼ teaspoon ginger

⅛ teaspoon ground cloves

⅛ teaspoon allspice

Preheat oven to 325°F. Press crust into a deep-dish pie plate and set aside.

In the bowl of a stand mixer fitted with the paddle attachment, beat cream cheese, butter, and sugar until light and fluffy, about 5 minutes. Add eggs, buttermilk, flour, and vanilla extract. Beat until fully combined and smooth. Scrape the bottom and sides of the bowl with a rubber spatula to ensure even mixing. Pour about ⅔ of the cheesecake mixture into a second bowl and set aside.

Add pumpkin purée and spices to the remaining cheesecake mixture. Mix on medium speed until fully combined. Scrape the bottom and sides of the bowl with a rubber spatula to ensure even mixing.

Dollop both cream cheese mixtures into the prepared crust, alternating between the plain mixture and the pumpkin mixture. Use a knife to swirl the batter into a marble effect. Bake for 40 to 45 minutes or until edges are set and center still jiggles just a little. Cool completely, then cover and refrigerate for at least 4 hours.

Serve with Cream Cheese Whipped Cream and garnish with Salted Caramel and Toffee Pecans.

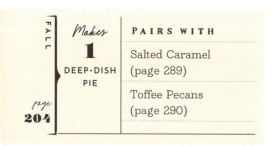

PAIRS WITH
Salted Caramel (page 289)
Toffee Pecans (page 290)

Pennie's Sweet Potato Pie

When my friend Rockelle talks about pie, sweet potato is what she always thinks about. This version of the Southern American holiday pie is based on Rockelle's family recipe. Every Thanksgiving and Christmas, Rockelle's mom, Pennie, makes six sweet potato pies, one for each of her six adult children. This pie is so beloved that each family member is gifted their own pie!

Roll out dough on a lightly floured surface to roughly a 13-inch round. Wrap loosely around rolling pin and transfer to a 9-inch pie plate. Cut off any extra crust and crimp edges. Loosely cover and refrigerate until ready to use.

Scrub potatoes and boil until fork tender with skin on, about 20 minutes. Remove from the water and allow to cool until you can handle them, then remove the skins. Preheat oven to 350°F.

Place cooked sweet potatoes in the bowl of a food processor with all of the remaining ingredients. Process until smooth.

Pour sweet potato mixture into the prepared crust. Use a pie shield or aluminum foil to cover the exposed edge of the crust to prevent burning. Bake for 1 hour or until the edges of the pie have mostly set and the center is a little jiggly. Allow the pie to cool completely, then cover and refrigerate for at least an hour before serving.

Single Butter Pie Dough (page 33)

1½ pounds (680 g) whole sweet potatoes

¼ cup (56 g) unsalted butter, melted

1 egg

¼ cup evaporated milk

¼ cup (50 g) sugar

1 ½ teaspoons cinnamon

¼ teaspoon nutmeg

1 tablespoon flour

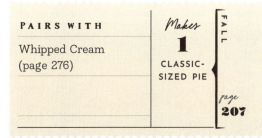

PAIRS WITH

Whipped Cream (page 276)

Makes
1
CLASSIC-SIZED PIE

FALL

Toffee Crumb Pie

This over-the-top, richly buttery pie is one of my dessert creations that I'm most proud of. I make it every Thanksgiving. The toffee melts into the filling as it bakes, making a gooey, chocolate, cookie-like center, jumbled with a slightly crisp crumb. Because the filling rises a bit and the crumb is heavy, the top of this pie comes out differently every time I bake it. Serve warm with Vanilla Bean Ice Cream.

Single Butter Pie Dough (page 33)

FILLING
¾ cup (169 g) unsalted butter, softened

1 cup (180 g) light brown sugar

2 eggs, room temperature

1 tablespoon vanilla extract

½ cup (65 g) all-purpose flour

½ teaspoon fine sea salt

8 ounces (227 g) toffee bar (with chocolate), chopped

CRUMB
¼ cup (56 g) unsalted butter

⅓ cup (59 g) light brown sugar

⅔ cup (86 g) all-purpose flour

¾ cup (130 g) mini semisweet chocolate chips

TO GARNISH
Whipped Cream (page 276)

¼ cup mini semisweet chocolate chips

¼ cup toffee bits

pie crust leaf cutouts

Chocolate Fudge Sauce (page 288)

Preheat oven to 375°F. Roll out dough on a lightly floured surface to roughly a 15-inch round. Wrap loosely around the rolling pin and transfer to a deep-dish pie plate. Cut off any extra crust and crimp edges.

To make the filling: In the bowl of a stand mixer fitted with the paddle attachment, beat butter and sugar on medium speed until light and fluffy, about 3 minutes. Add eggs and vanilla and beat until fully incorporated. In a small bowl, whisk together flour and salt. Add to butter mixture and mix just until combined. Scrape sides and bottom of bowl to ensure even mixing. Add chopped toffee and mix just until combined. Transfer filling to prepared crust.

To make the crumb: In a medium heatproof bowl, melt butter. Add brown sugar and flour; stir to combine. If the mixture is still hot, allow to cool until the chocolate chips are in no danger of melting before adding them, and stir to combine. Crumble the crumb mixture evenly over the filling. If using pie crust leaf cutouts to garnish, add them now.

Bake for 45 to 50 minutes or until top is golden brown. Allow pie to cool for 20 to 30 minutes before cutting. Serve warm with desired garnishes and Vanilla Bean Ice Cream.

❋ *This pie also freezes well. Cut cooled pie into pieces and store in a freezer bag in the freezer for up to 2 months. To revive frozen pie pieces, place on a parchment-lined baking sheet in a preheated 275°F oven for 12 to 15 minutes.*

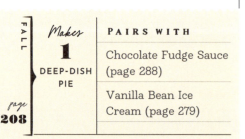

FALL

Makes
1
DEEP-DISH PIE

PAIRS WITH

Chocolate Fudge Sauce (page 288)

Vanilla Bean Ice Cream (page 279)

Enchilada Pie

This red enchilada sauce is based on my mother's recipe, which our family adored. This pie is like a stacked enchilada with layers of beef, refried black beans, and cheese. It's a comforting hot pie and makes a perfect family meal.

ENCHILADA SAUCE

4 dried Anaheim chili peppers

1 sm. (125 g) sweet onion, chopped

¾ teaspoon fine sea salt

2 teaspoons cumin

2 teaspoons chili powder

1 clove garlic, minced

¾ cup water

3 tablespoons vegetable oil

1 (28 ounce) can tomato sauce

BEEF

1 pound (454 g) lean ground beef

½ cup water

1 tablespoon dried minced onion

1 tablespoon chili powder

½ teaspoon garlic powder

1 teaspoon ground cumin

½ teaspoon dried oregano

1 teaspoon fine sea salt

½ teaspoon freshly ground black pepper

REFRIED BLACK BEANS

½ med. white onion, finely chopped

2 tablespoons olive or vegetable oil

1 (15 ounce) can black beans

To make the enchilada sauce: Soak chili peppers in water until soft, about 1 hour. Remove stems and seeds from softened chilies and place peppers in the pitcher of a blender with onion, salt, cumin, chili powder, garlic, and water. Blend until puréed.

In a large saucepan over medium-high heat, add vegetable oil. When oil is hot, carefully pour in the chili pepper mixture. Add tomato sauce, stir, and cook for 5 minutes.

To cook the beef: Brown ground beef in a skillet over medium-high heat until fully cooked. Drain off excess fat. Add water to the skillet and bring to a simmer. In a small bowl, combine all of the seasonings and add to the skillet. Stir to evenly distribute and simmer for about 3 more minutes.

To make the refried black beans: In a large skillet, heat oil over medium heat. Add onions and cook until golden, about 8 minutes. Add undrained beans to the skillet. While cooking, carefully blend beans with an immersion blender until smooth. If you don't have an immersion blender, use a potato masher. Mash until the beans are as smooth as you can get them. After blended, continue to cook beans until they have reached your desired thickness. Use a rubber spatula to scrape the bottom of the skillet as you cook to prevent beans from sticking.

To assemble: Preheat oven to 350°F. Add a thin layer of sauce to the bottom of a deep-dish pie plate. Dip 1 tortilla in the sauce and add to the pie plate; top with half of the ground beef. Dip another tortilla in sauce and place over ground beef. Top with half of the refried beans. Dip another tortilla in sauce and place over beans. Top with 1 cup of the cheese. Repeat each layer. Add tortilla number 7 to the top. Generously cover with remaining enchilada sauce. Place pie on a rimmed baking sheet to catch drips and cover with foil. Bake for 15 minutes, then remove foil and sprinkle with remaining 1 cup cheese. Bake for an additional 25 to 30 minutes or until sauce and cheese are bubbling. Sprinkle with fresh cilantro and serve.

FALL

Makes

1

DEEP-DISH PIE

TO ASSEMBLE

7 9-inch tortillas

3 cups Colby Jack cheese

¼ cup chopped fresh cilantro

❋ If you don't have time to make your own sauce, you can replace with 30 ounces of your favorite storebought red enchilada sauce.

❋ A straight-edged deep-dish pie plate works best for this pie so there is enough room for the bottom layers of tortillas to lie flat. If you only have a tapered pie plate, allow the bottom tortillas to curve along the edge of the dish.

Samosa Pie

Samosas are flavor-packed South Asian street snacks with a long history that have become popular around the world. I created this dish as a way to get that amazing aroma and taste into a pie, though I took some liberties and picked up elements from some of the best of my friend Mumtaz's Pakistani recipes for this beautifully spiced and comforting pie. The Cilantro Mint Chutney is an optional accompaniment I heartily recommend. It's easy to make and adds more depth to this already flavorful pie.

Double Butter Pie Dough (page 33)

POTATO FILLING
1 pound (454 g) yellow potatoes, peeled and washed

3 tablespoons butter, melted

fine sea salt to taste

½ teaspoon chili powder

¼ cup chopped cilantro

CHICKEN FILLING
¼ cup ghee (or clarified butter)

1 sm. white onion, finely chopped

2 cloves garlic, minced

1 jalapeño pepper, cored, seeded, and finely chopped

1 pound ground chicken

fine sea salt to taste

½ teaspoon ground ginger

1 teaspoon crushed red pepper

½ teaspoon chili powder

¼ teaspoon garam masala

2 teaspoons ground cumin

1 teaspoon ground coriander

1 cup frozen peas

¼ cup chopped cilantro

Egg Wash (page 275)

Divide double pie dough, reserving ⅓ for the top crust and ⅔ for the bottom crust. On a lightly floured surface, roll out the larger portion of dough to a roughly 17-inch circle. Wrap loosely around the rolling pin and carefully place in a 9-inch springform pan, covering the bottom and sides. Take care not to puncture the dough, which can cause leaking while the filling bakes. Loosely cover with plastic wrap and place in the refrigerator while making the filling.

To make the filling: Boil potatoes until tender. Use a ricer or a potato masher to mash potatoes. Add butter, salt, chili powder, and cilantro and stir to thoroughly combine.

In a large skillet over medium heat, melt ghee. Add onions and cook until translucent, about 5 minutes. Add garlic and continue cooking until fragrant. Add jalapeño, ground chicken, salt, and spices. Cook, stirring constantly, until the chicken has cooked through. Turn off heat and stir in peas and cilantro.

To assemble: Preheat oven to 375°F. When filling has cooled, roll out the second half of the dough on a lightly floured surface. Uncover bottom crust and add about half of the potatoes, then top with half of the chicken mixture. Repeat one more layer of each filling. Top with the second crust. Cut off any extra crust and attach top crust to the bottom crust and crimp edges. Brush the top with Egg Wash and cut vents into the top crust. Bake for 1 hour and 5 minutes or until the top is golden brown and the filling is cooked all the way through. Remove the sides of the springform pan and serve hot.

F A L L

Makes
1
9-INCH
SPRINGFORM
PIE
G✳F

page
212

CILANTRO MINT CHUTNEY

1 cup packed fresh cilantro leaves

¾ cup packed fresh mint leaves

1 jalapeño pepper, cored, seeded, and finely chopped

1 clove garlic

1 teaspoon ground cumin

½ teaspoon sugar

¼ cup walnuts

½ teaspoon fine sea salt

2 tablespoons fresh lime juice

⅓ cup water

To make the Cilantro Mint Chutney: In the bowl of a food processor, blend all ingredients until smooth. Serve as a side to go with the Samosa Pie.

Lemon Chicken Shepherd's Pie

I wanted to create a twist on a typical shepherd's pie, which usually has beef or lamb, and make it with chicken, lemon, and rosemary, my favorite flavors to pair with roast chicken. Topped with mashed potatoes, this hearty, creamy pie is a great comfort meal on a cold autumn day.

Preheat oven to 350°F. Peel potatoes and roughly chop if large. Boil in water over medium-high heat until tender.

While potatoes are cooking, make the filling: In a 3½-quart braiser or large oven-safe skillet, melt butter over medium heat. Whisk in flour and continue to stir until a thick paste forms. Add heavy cream and lemon juice and whisk until all lumps have dissolved. Add chicken broth and cheese and whisk until a smooth sauce forms. Mix in thyme, rosemary, and vegetables; stir with rubber spatula until vegetables are fully coated in sauce. Lay lemon slices on top and increase temperature to medium-high. Once the mixture begins to bubble, reduce temperature to medium and cook for 5 more minutes. Remove from heat, discard the lemon slices, and add chicken. Stir until chicken is coated.

To make the topping: Drain potatoes and return them to the stove on low heat. Add butter, half and half, cheese, salt, and pepper. Blend with a hand mixer or potato masher until cheese is melted and all ingredients are fully incorporated. Turn off heat and stir in chives and parsley. Dollop mashed potatoes onto chicken mixture and spread evenly across the top of the pie. Bake until potatoes start to turn golden brown and the filling is bubbling at the edges, about 50 minutes. Serve immediately.

✻ *If you have a ricer, you can pass the cooked potatoes through the ricer and then stir in the other potato ingredients for an even better texture.*

FILLING

¼ cup (56 g) salted butter

½ cup (65 g) all-purpose flour

½ cup heavy cream

¼ cup fresh lemon juice

2 cups chicken broth

2 ounces (57 g) Gouda cheese, shredded

fine sea salt and pepper, to taste

1 teaspoon fresh thyme leaves

2 teaspoons finely chopped fresh rosemary

2 cups (280 g) mixed vegetables, such as corn, peas, and carrots

½ lemon, sliced

4 cups (400 g) pulled rotisserie chicken

POTATO TOPPING

2 pounds (907 g) all-purpose potatoes

¼ cup (56 g) salted butter, melted

¾ cup half and half

2 ounces (57 g) Gouda cheese, shredded

fine sea salt and pepper to taste

2 tablespoons chopped chives

2 tablespoons chopped fresh parsley

Makes **1** SKILLET PIE

FALL

Chuchito Pie

Chuchitos are a traditional Guatemalan tamale, popular to eat for breakfast. They make great snacks and I love to grab one any time of the day when I'm visiting. Chicken with a homemade red sauce is packed inside corn masa dough that is then wrapped in corn husks and steamed. My sister-in-law taught me her recipe, which I have used to make them at home. The process of creating them is a little too labor intensive for me, and I've found that the same flavors come together much easier in the form of a pie. Though not the neat little package of a real chuchito, this pie has won over my Guatemalan family for its flavors, reminding them of home.

FILLING

2 medium (300 g) tomatoes

2 dried Anaheim chili peppers

2 cloves garlic

¼ cup raw pepitas

¼ cup sesame seeds

½ teaspoon ground cumin

¼ teaspoon allspice

¼ teaspoon ground black pepper

2 teaspoons fine sea salt

1 pound boneless, skinless chicken breast

MASA

2¾ cups (290 g) masa harina

2 teaspoons fine sea salt

¼ cup (56 g) unsalted butter, melted

1¾ cups water

4-5 dried corn husks, optional

Submerge corn husks in water, if using, and allow to soak while preparing the pie.

Core and quarter tomatoes. Add to a medium saucepan with enough water to cover. Remove the stems and seeds from the dried chili peppers and add peppers to the saucepan. Add garlic cloves and bring water to a boil over medium-high heat. Continue to cook until the tomatoes are tender, about 20 minutes.

In a medium frying pan, toast pepitas, sesame seeds, cumin, allspice, and black pepper over medium heat until seeds are lightly browned, about 4 minutes. Stir continuously to avoid burning.

Preheat oven to 350°F. Set a deep-dish pie plate on a rimmed baking sheet.

Use a slotted spoon to add tomatoes, chilies, and garlic to the pitcher of a blender. Add toasted seeds and spices, salt, and 1 cup of the tomato cooking water. Blend on high until ingredients are completely liquefied and you can no longer see the seeds, about 1 minute. Dice chicken and place in the prepared pie plate. Pour sauce over chicken and stir to coat.

To make the masa: In the bowl of a stand mixer fitted with the paddle attachment, add masa harina and salt. Mix on low to distribute salt. Add melted butter and water and mix on low for 2 minutes. Dollop masa on top of chicken mixture to cover as much of the top as possible. Cover masa with damp corn husks, if using, and cover the entire pie with foil. Bake for 1 hour and 10 minutes. Remove foil and corn husks and serve immediately.

FALL

Makes

1

DEEP-DISH PIE

G✳F

page
216

Winter

Peppermint Mocha Pie

Peppermint and chocolate are a beautiful combination that always reminds me of the holiday season. With a brownie-like filling topped with peppermint cream, this pie hits the spot and will fill you and your guests with Christmas cheer. You might skip the cookies for Santa and leave out a slice of this chocolatey pie instead.

Preheat oven to 425°F. Roll out dough on a lightly floured surface to roughly a 15-inch round. Wrap loosely around the rolling pin and transfer to a 9-inch pie plate. Cut off any extra crust and crimp edges. Parbake the crust using the instructions on page 41. Reduce oven temperature to 350°F. (If using crumb crust, press into pie plate and set aside.)

To make the filling: Melt chocolate and allow to cool. In the bowl of a stand mixer fitted with the paddle attachment, beat butter, sugars, and vanilla extract on medium speed until light and fluffy, about 4 minutes. Add eggs one at a time, beating between each addition. Scrape the sides and bottom of the bowl to ensure even mixing. Add cooled melted chocolate to the butter mixture. Beat until well combined. Remove bowl from mixer.

In a medium bowl, whisk together flour, cocoa, espresso powder, and salt. Sift into butter mixture. With a rubber spatula, stir by hand just until combined. Pour into prepared crust. Bake for 25 to 30 minutes or until the edges have set and the center is still a little jiggly.

Just before serving, make Peppermint Whipped Cream: In the bowl of a stand mixer fitted with the whisk attachment, add cream cheese and heavy cream. Beat on medium speed for 4 to 5 minutes or until stiff peaks form. Add confectioners' sugar and peppermint extract. Mix until combined. Add to the top of the cooled pie with an offset spatula or pipe on with a pastry bag. Garnish as desired and serve immediately with Chocolate Fudge Sauce.

❁ *To create festive stripes on piped peppermint whipped cream, paint red food coloring on the inside of the pastry bag from tip to opening before adding whipped cream to the bag.*

Single Chocolate Pie Dough (page 35) or Classic Chocolate Wafer Crumb Crust (page 52)

FILLING
5 ounces (142 g) dark chocolate, coarsely chopped

¼ cup (56 g) butter, softened

¾ cup (150 g) sugar

¾ cup (135 g) brown sugar

1 tablespoon vanilla extract

3 eggs

¼ cup (33 g) all-purpose flour

2 tablespoons unsweetened cocoa powder

1½ tablespoons espresso powder

¼ teaspoon fine sea salt

PEPPERMINT WHIPPED CREAM
8 ounces (227 g) cold cream cheese

1¾ cups heavy cream

1 cup (110 g) confectioners' sugar

½ teaspoon peppermint extract

TO GARNISH
holiday themed silver and white sprinkles

chopped peppermint candy canes

PAIRS WITH

Chocolate Fudge Sauce (page 288)

Makes
1
CLASSIC-SIZED PIE

WINTER

White Chocolate Cranberry Tart

At Christmas, when everything is just a little more decorated and special than any other time of the year, this lovely tart makes a beautiful addition to a dessert spread when ornamented with red cranberries and green rosemary. The tart filling complements the sweet white chocolate and is a seasonal treat.

Press-In Shortbread Tart Dough (page 49)

CRANBERRY FILLING

2½ cups (250 g) fresh cranberries

⅔ cup (132 g) sugar

1½ tablespoons cornstarch

⅛ teaspoon fine sea salt

1 tablespoon fresh lemon juice

⅓ cup maple syrup

GANACHE TOPPING

5 ounces (141 g) white chocolate, chopped

½ cup heavy cream

TO GARNISH

fresh rosemary sprigs

Sugared Cranberries (page 285)

White Chocolate Curls (page 293)

To make the crust: Preheat oven to 350°F. Press tart dough into a 10-inch tart pan. Generously dock with a fork and bake for 25 to 30 minutes or until lightly browned. While still hot, use a tamper or the back of a spoon to lightly press down the center of the crust, leaving a ¾-inch edge.

To make the cranberry filling: In the bowl of a food processor, finely chop cranberries. In a small bowl, whisk together sugar, cornstarch, and salt. Add to the food processor and pulse to combine. In a medium saucepan, combine lemon juice, maple syrup, and cranberry mixture. Cook over medium-high heat. When the mixture starts to bubble, reduce temperature to medium. Continue cooking until most of the cranberries have broken down and juices have thickened, about 10 minutes. Add to the prepared crust. Cover and refrigerate for at least 30 minutes.

To make the ganache: Add chopped chocolate to a heatproof bowl. Heat heavy cream over medium-high heat until steaming but not boiling. Remove from heat. Pour cream over chocolate and allow to sit for about 1 minute. Using a rubber spatula, stir until chocolate is melted and fully incorporated. Allow ganache to sit for 5 to 10 minutes, until it thickens a little, then pour over cooled tart filling. Cover and refrigerate for 1 hour or until ganache sets before removing from tart pan. Keep in the refrigerator until ready to serve. Garnish tart just before serving.

Makes
1
10-INCH
TART

G✳F

PAIRS WITH

White Chocolate Curls (page 293)

Sugared Cranberries (page 285)

Cranberry Apple Pie

When the fresh cranberries show up in the grocery store, I start thinking of Thanksgiving and Christmas baking. The cranberries turn this apple pie a deep red and add a bright tart flavor, perfect for the holidays. You can customize the top crust with cutouts to bring out the season. Serve warm topped with ice cream.

To make the filling: In the bowl of a food processor, combine cranberries, sugar, lemon juice, and cornstarch. Process until cranberries are finely chopped and all ingredients are incorporated. Set aside.

In a medium mixing bowl, whisk together brown sugar, cinnamon, and cardamom. Add apples and stir until evenly coated. Add cranberry mixture to apples and stir until cranberries are evenly distributed.

To make the crust: Roll out the first disk of dough on a lightly floured surface to roughly a 15-inch round. Wrap loosely around the rolling pin and transfer to a deep-dish pie plate. Cut off any extra crust. Fill with apple cranberry mixture. Roll out the second portion of dough and assemble the crust using your desired top crust method (see pages 42-47). Crimp top and bottom crust together. Cut vents in the top crust. Loosely cover the pie and refrigerate for 30 minutes to 1 hour.

Preheat oven to 375°F. Brush the top crust of the pie evenly with Egg Wash. Sprinkle with turbinado sugar. Bake for 45 to 50 minutes or until the filling is bubbling and the crust is golden brown. Allow pie to rest for 15 minutes and serve warm with Vanilla Bean Ice Cream or Whipped Cream.

❉ *To revive cold pie, preheat oven to 300°F and warm for 10 to 20 minutes.*

Double Butter Pie Dough (page 33)

2 cups (200 g) fresh cranberries

¼ cup (50 g) sugar

1 tablespoon fresh lemon juice

1 tablespoon cornstarch

1 cup (180 g) brown sugar

1 teaspoon cinnamon

½ teaspoon cardamom

4 cups (500 g) peeled, cored, and sliced apples (about 4)

½ cup chopped walnuts

2 tablespoons maple syrup

1 tablespoon vanilla bean paste

Egg Wash (page 275)

2 tablespoons turbinado sugar

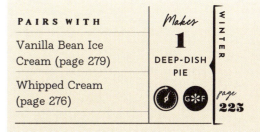

PAIRS WITH

Vanilla Bean Ice Cream (page 279)

Whipped Cream (page 276)

Makes
1
DEEP-DISH
PIE

WINTER

page
227

Spiced Gingerbread Tart

This festive tart with a gingerbread-spiced crust is a fun addition to any Christmas celebration. With so many warm seasonal spices and an ornamented top with gingerbread cutouts and Sugared Cranberries, it may just become one of your holiday traditions.

GINGERBREAD PRESS-IN CRUST

1 cup (225 g) unsalted butter, softened

2 teaspoons vanilla extract

½ cup (90 g) brown sugar

3 tablespoons unsulfured molasses

3 cups (345 g) pastry or cake flour

½ teaspoon fine sea salt

1 teaspoon cinnamon

½ teaspoon ginger

¼ teaspoon cloves

¼ teaspoon allspice

FILLING

4 ounces (114 g) cold cream cheese

1 tablespoon vanilla bean paste

1 teaspoon cinnamon

½ teaspoon nutmeg

⅔ cup (73 g) confectioners' sugar

1 cup heavy cream

TO GARNISH

Sugared Cranberries (page 285)

fresh rosemary sprigs

To make the crust: In the bowl of a stand mixer fitted with the paddle attachment, mix butter, vanilla, brown sugar, and molasses on high until light and fluffy, about 5 minutes. In a medium bowl, whisk together flour, salt, and spices. Add to the butter mixture and mix just until combined.

Preheat oven to 350°F. Press about ⅔ of the tart dough into a 10-inch tart pan. Generously dock with a fork and bake for 20 to 25 minutes. Allow to cool completely.

To make the filling: In the bowl of a stand mixer fitted with the whisk attachment, beat cream cheese, vanilla bean paste, cinnamon, nutmeg, and confectioners' sugar on medium speed until light, fluffy, and smooth, about 5 minutes. With the mixer running on low, slowly add heavy cream. Once cream is incorporated, increase speed to high. Continue beating until stiff peaks form, about 5 minutes. Add filling to cooled crust. Spread with an offset spatula, making the surface as smooth as possible. Cover and refrigerate until ready to serve.

To make the gingerbread cookie garnish: Preheat oven to 350°F. Line a baking sheet with parchment paper or a silicone baking mat. On a lightly floured surface, roll out remaining tart dough. Use cookie cutters to create cutouts. Place on prepared pan and bake for 10 to 12 minutes.

To serve: Remove tart from pan and top with gingerbread cookies, Sugared Cranberries, and fresh rosemary sprigs.

WINTER

Makes
1
10-INCH TART

PAIRS WITH

Sugared Cranberries (page 285)

Peppermint Icebox Pie

This pretty, light, and fluffy peppermint icebox pie is a refreshing wintertime treat that is perfect for a Christmas party with its cute candy stripe garnish and pink filling.

Preheat oven to 350°F. Press crust into a deep-dish pie plate and bake for 6 minutes. Allow to cool.

To make the filling: In the bowl of a stand mixer fitted with the whisk attachment, beat cream cheese until fluffy, about 4 minutes. Add marshmallow fluff, confectioners' sugar, and extracts and mix until combined. Scrape sides and bottom of bowl to ensure even mixing. Add heavy cream and beat on high until soft peaks form. Add pink food coloring and mix on low just to combine. Pour filling into the cooled crust. For swirls, add some red food coloring gel to a toothpick and swirl into the filling. Cover and refrigerate at least 2 hours.

Garnish with Whipped Cream and crushed peppermint candies just before serving.

Deep-Dish Chocolate Wafer Crumb Crust (page 52)

FILLING

8 ounces (227 g) cold cream cheese

7 ounces (198 g) marshmallow fluff

¾ cup (83 g) confectioners' sugar

2 teaspoons vanilla extract

1 teaspoon peppermint extract

1½ cups heavy cream

4 drops pink food coloring gel

1 drop red food coloring gel

TO GARNISH

Whipped Cream (page 276)

crushed peppermint candies or candy canes

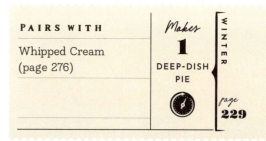

PAIRS WITH

Whipped Cream (page 276)

Makes
1
DEEP-DISH PIE

WINTER

Shoofly Pie

Originating as a kind of molasses coffee cake, shoofly pie was made popular by the Pennsylvania Dutch and got its unique name from a brand of molasses–which got its name from a mule in a traveling circus. The main filling in the pie is so runny when it goes in the oven that it seems like it could never firm up, but the crumb topping and baking transform the filling into a deliciously spiced pie. The pie was historically eaten year-round and was a popular breakfast baked good. To me, the flavors are reminiscent of Christmas, making this more of a holiday pie on my baking list.

Preheat oven to 450°F. Roll out dough on a lightly floured surface to roughly a 15-inch round. Wrap loosely around the rolling pin and transfer to a deep-dish pie plate. Cut off any extra crust and crimp edges. Place in the refrigerator while making the filling.

To make the filling: In the bowl of a stand mixer fitted with the whisk attachment, add egg, molasses, maple syrup, vanilla extract, salt, and baking soda. Beat on medium speed until fully incorporated, about 2 minutes. Add boiling water slowly and continue to mix on low while making the crumb.

To make the crumb: In the bowl of a food processor, add flour, brown sugar, and spices. Pulse to combine. Cut cold butter into slices and add to the flour mixture. Process until a fine crumb forms.

Pour the molasses mixture into the prepared pie crust. Sprinkle the crumb over the top, mounding it slightly in the center. Place pie on a rimmed baking sheet to catch any drips. Bake for 10 minutes at 450°F, then reduce the oven temperature to 350°F and bake for an additional 30 minutes or until the crumb is golden and the pie has set. Allow to cool completely before cutting. Serve with Vanilla Bean Ice Cream.

Single Butter Pie Dough (page 33)

FILLING
1 egg

½ cup unsulfured molasses

¼ cup maple syrup

2 teaspoons vanilla extract

⅛ teaspoon fine sea salt

1 teaspoon baking soda

¾ cup boiling water

CRUMB
1⅔ cups (217 g) all-purpose flour

1 cup (180 g) dark brown sugar

1 teaspoon cinnamon

¼ teaspoon nutmeg

⅛ teaspoon ginger

⅛ teaspoon cloves

10 tablespoons (141 g) unsalted butter, cold

PAIRS WITH

Vanilla Bean Ice Cream (page 279)

Makes

1

DEEP-DISH PIE

WINTER

Magic Pie

Based on a long-standing Christmas essential recipe my friend Allison made every year during our holiday baking marathons, Magic Pie has all of the irresistible flavors of magic bars in a thicker, richer, cookie-like pie form. This is a delight for a Christmas or Thanksgiving dessert.

Deep-Dish Graham Cracker Crumb Crust (page 52)

FILLING

½ cup (113 g) salted butter, softened

½ cup (90 g) brown sugar

1 egg

1 teaspoon vanilla extract

½ cup (65 g) all-purpose flour

¾ cup (135 g) milk chocolate chips

¾ cup (135 g) white chocolate chips

¾ cup (135 g) dark chocolate chips

¾ cup (117 g) chopped toffee bar

½ cup (53 g) chopped pecans

1 (14 ounce) can sweetened condensed milk

2 cups (200 g) sweetened flake coconut

Preheat oven to 350°F. Press crust into a deep-dish pie plate and set aside.

In the bowl of a stand mixer, mix butter, brown sugar, egg, and vanilla on high until light and fluffy, about 4 minutes. Add flour and mix just until combined. Pour into the prepared crust and spread evenly. Sprinkle chocolate chips, toffee, and pecans over the mixture. Pour sweetened condensed milk evenly over top and sprinkle with coconut. Place the pie on a rimmed baking sheet to catch any drips. Bake for 45 to 50 minutes or until the coconut is golden brown.

Allow to cool completely before cutting. Serve with Whipped Cream and Salted Caramel.

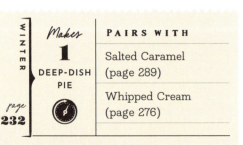

WINTER

Makes
1
DEEP-DISH PIE

PAIRS WITH

Salted Caramel (page 289)

Whipped Cream (page 276)

Blackberry Chocolate Mini Pies

These cute mini pies can be customized with crust cutouts and make a nice addition to a Christmas treat tray or dessert spread.

To make the blackberry filling: In a medium bowl, whisk together sugar, cornstarch, and salt. In a medium saucepan, add blackberries, vanilla, and sugar mixture. Cook over medium heat until the berries start to break down. Continue cooking, stirring frequently, until the filling has thickened and coats the back of a spoon, about 6 minutes. Allow to come to room temperature.

To make the brownie filling: In the bowl of a stand mixer fitted with the whisk attachment, beat melted butter and brown sugar on medium speed until combined. Add eggs one at a time, mixing between each addition. Add vanilla and melted chocolate and mix just until combined. Remove bowl from the stand mixer. In a medium bowl, sift together cocoa, flour, and salt, then whisk to combine. Add to the butter mixture and stir by hand with a rubber spatula just until combined.

To assemble: Start with about ⅔ of the crust dough. Wrap and refrigerate the remaining dough. Divide the larger portion into 6 equal portions. Roll each to about a 7-inch circle and place in the mini pie plates. Cut off any extra crust. Divide the brownie batter between the 6 mini pies. Top with the cooled blackberry filling. Roll out remaining crust to make cutouts or lattice tops. Connect the top crust to the bottom and crimp edges. Brush with Egg Wash.

Place the mini pies on a rimmed baking sheet and refrigerate for 20 minutes before baking. Preheat oven to 400°F. Bake pies for 30 to 35 minutes or until crust is golden brown and filling is bubbling. Allow to cool for 20 minutes before serving with Whipped Cream or Vanilla Bean Ice Cream.

SPECIAL EQUIPMENT
6 5-inch mini pie plates

Extra-Large Butter Pie Dough (page 33)

BERRY FILLING
½ cup (100 g) sugar

1 tablespoon cornstarch

½ teaspoon fine sea salt

2 cups (252 g) fresh blackberries (or thawed frozen)

1 teaspoon vanilla extract

BROWNIE FILLING
½ cup (113 g) unsalted butter, melted and cooled

¾ cup (135 g) brown sugar

2 eggs, room temperature

1 tablespoon vanilla extract

2 ounces (57 g) bittersweet chocolate, melted and cooled

⅓ cup (30 g) unsweetened cocoa powder

¼ cup (33 g) all-purpose flour

½ teaspoon fine sea salt

Egg Wash (page 275)

PAIRS WITH

Whipped Cream (page 276)

Vanilla Bean Ice Cream (page 279)

Makes
6
MINI PIES

WINTER

Raspberry Linzer Tart

Linzer tortes have been made in Linz, Austria, for centuries. With an almond crust and raspberry filling, this tart based on the popular holiday torte is also similar to Linzer cookies, another Christmastime favorite. You will love the delicate, slightly crisp crust with the jammy filling.

ALMOND CRUST

½ cup whole raw almonds

1 cup (225 g) unsalted butter, softened

1 cup (200 g) sugar

1 teaspoon vanilla extract

2 eggs, room temperature

2¾ cups (358 g) all-purpose flour

1 teaspoon baking powder

½ teaspoon fine sea salt

½ teaspoon cinnamon

1½ cups Raspberry Jam (page 286)

Sweet Egg Wash (page 275)

confectioners' sugar, to garnish

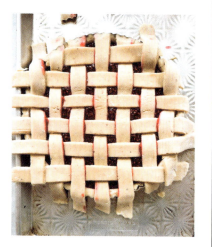

Preheat oven to 350°F. Place almonds on a single layer on a rimmed baking sheet, bake 7 minutes, remove, and allow to cool.

In the bowl of a stand mixer fitted with the paddle attachment, beat butter, sugar, and vanilla for 2 to 3 minutes on medium speed until fluffy. Add eggs and beat until combined.

In a food processor, process cooled almonds until fine. Add flour, baking powder, salt, and cinnamon. Pulse until well combined. Add flour mixture to the butter mixture and beat on medium speed until well combined.

Divide dough into two portions. Wrap each portion in plastic wrap and refrigerate for at least 30 minutes or overnight.

When ready to bake, preheat oven to 350°F. On a lightly floured surface, roll out the first portion of the dough to about a 12-inch round. Place in a 10-inch tart pan. If dough cracks while moving it, simply press cracks together. Pour jam into the crust. Roll out the second portion of dough, cut into strips, and form a lattice top (see page 42).

Place tart on a rimmed baking sheet and bake for 40 to 45 minutes or until crust is golden and filling is bubbling. Dust with confectioners' sugar and serve warm with Whipped Cream.

✱ *This recipe makes ample dough for forming the long strips necessary for making the lattice top. If you have extra dough, you can use it to embellish your crust or roll it out, cut it into rounds, and bake on a baking sheet at 350°F for 10 to 13 minutes.*

WINTER

Makes

1

10-INCH
TART

PAIRS WITH

Whipped Cream
(page 276)

Kitchen Sink Pie

My son, who loves all things sweet and salty, is a huge fan of kitchen sink cookies, which inspired me to turn the concept into a pie. This fun pie has a little bit of so many snackable treats, making it gooey and crunchy and salty and sweet. Try it warm with Vanilla Bean Ice Cream and Chocolate Fudge Sauce for an irresistible dessert.

Press the crust into a deep-dish pie plate and set aside.

To make the filling: In the bowl of a stand mixer fitted with the paddle attachment, beat butter and sugar on medium speed until light and fluffy, about 3 minutes. Add eggs and vanilla and beat until fully incorporated. In a small bowl, whisk together flour and salt. Add to butter mixture and mix just until combined. Scrape sides and bottom of bowl to ensure even mixing. Add walnuts, chocolate, toffee, peanut butter cups, and caramel bits and stir by hand just until combined.

Pour filling into the prepared crust and top with pretzels. Bake for 40 to 45 minutes or until the top of the pie is golden brown, the edges have started to set, and the center is still a little jiggly. Allow the pie to cool for 20 to 30 minutes before cutting. Serve warm with Vanilla Bean Ice Cream and Chocolate Fudge Sauce.

Deep-Dish Pretzel Crumb Crust (page 52)

FILLING

1 cup (225 g) unsalted butter, softened

1¼ cups (225 g) light brown sugar

3 eggs, room temperature

1 tablespoon vanilla extract

¾ cup (98 g) all-purpose flour

½ teaspoon fine sea salt

½ cup (60 g) chopped walnuts

4 ounces semisweet chocolate, coarsely chopped

½ cup white chocolate chips

½ cup chopped toffee bar

½ cup coarsely chopped peanut butter cups

½ cup caramel bits

1 cup pretzels

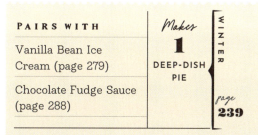

PAIRS WITH

Vanilla Bean Ice Cream (page 279)

Chocolate Fudge Sauce (page 288)

Makes
1
DEEP-DISH
PIE

WINTER

Mint Chocolate Ice Cream Pie

Mint chocolate chip ice cream has long been a top choice for me, and the holidays seem to be one of the best times to bring out mint flavor. The homemade ice cream filling is flavored with crème de menthe syrup, which gives it a lovely level of mintiness without being overpowering. The mint complements the dark chocolate and chocolate crust, making a refreshing and pretty winter pie.

SPECIAL EQUIPMENT
Ice Cream Maker

Classic Chocolate Wafer Crumb Crust (page 52)

1¾ cups heavy cream

1¾ cups whole milk, divided

2 tablespoons cornstarch

¾ cup crème de menthe syrup

1 tablespoon vanilla bean paste

1 cup Dark Chocolate Curls (page 293), plus more to garnish

¼ cup Chocolate Fudge Sauce (page 288), plus more to garnish

In a large pot over medium-high heat, whisk together heavy cream and 1½ cups milk. In a small bowl, combine remaining ¼ cup milk with cornstarch. Mix until all lumps have dissolved and add to the pot. Add crème de menthe and vanilla bean paste and whisk to combine. Continue cooking until the mixture just about reaches a boil. Reduce heat to medium-low and continue cooking until mixture thickens, about 5 more minutes. Allow to cool, then cover and chill in the refrigerator for at least 2 hours or overnight.

To make the crust: Preheat oven to 350°F. Press crumb crust into a 9-inch pie plate and bake for 6 minutes. If the crust slips down the sides of the pan while baking, use a tamper or the back of a spoon to press the crust back up the sides of the pan. Allow to cool completely.

Add chilled cream mixture to an ice cream maker and follow manufacturer's instructions to churn into ice cream. When ice cream is finished, mix in the Chocolate Curls and scoop into the pie crust. Swirl in Chocolate Fudge Sauce. Cover and freeze for at least 2 hours or overnight. When ready to serve, garnish with more Chocolate Curls and Chocolate Fudge Sauce.

❋ *One of the easiest ways to cut this pie is to pop it out of the pie plate, place the pie on a cutting board, and cut it with a large chef's knife. Serve cut pieces immediately or return them to pie plate, cover, and store in the freezer.*

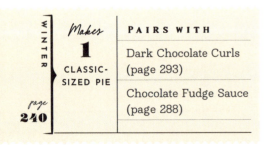

WINTER

Makes
1
CLASSIC-SIZED PIE

PAIRS WITH

Dark Chocolate Curls (page 293)

Chocolate Fudge Sauce (page 288)

Fluffernutter Brownie Pie

Marshmallow fluff and peanut butter combine to make the kid-classic sweet sandwich. Turns out those two flavors also go great with brownies. This sweet and pretty pie is a tasty addition to a party and a great way to get kids involved in baking.

Parbake crust in a deep-dish pie plate according to the instructions on page 41. Reduce oven temperature to 350°F.

To make the brownie filling: In the bowl of a stand mixer fitted with the whisk attachment, beat melted butter and sugars until combined. Add eggs one at a time, mixing between each addition. Add vanilla and melted chocolate and mix just until combined. Remove bowl from the stand mixer. In a medium bowl, sift together cocoa, flour, and salt, then whisk to combine. Add to the butter mixture and stir by hand with a rubber spatula just until combined. Add to the parbaked crust.

In a heatproof bowl, warm peanut butter in the microwave in 20-second intervals, or until it becomes fluid and easy to pour. Repeat the process with marshmallow fluff. Dollop peanut butter and marshmallow fluff onto the top of the brownie batter in an alternating pattern. Use a butter knife to swirl the fillings.

Bake for 30 to 35 minutes or until edges have set and center is slightly jiggly. Allow to cool for at least 30 minutes before cutting. Serve with Vanilla Bean Ice Cream.

Single Butter Pie Dough (page 33)

¾ cup (169 g) unsalted butter, melted and cooled

½ cup (90 g) brown sugar

½ cup (100 g) sugar

3 eggs, room temperature

1 teaspoon vanilla extract

2 ounces (57 g) bittersweet chocolate, melted and cooled

⅓ cup (30 g) unsweetened cocoa powder

¼ cup (33 g) all-purpose flour

½ teaspoon fine sea salt

¾ cup (192 g) smooth peanut butter

7 ounces (198 g) marshmallow fluff

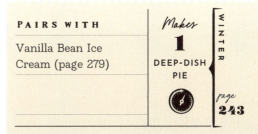

PAIRS WITH

Vanilla Bean Ice Cream (page 279)

Makes
1
DEEP-DISH
PIE

WINTER

Cookie Dough Tart

When we were kids, my brother used to drop an entire cookie scoop of dough directly into his mouth whenever I was baking chocolate chip cookies. I admit to enjoying a taste or two of the dough myself. It's probably not the best idea to eat too much, though, with raw egg and uncooked flour. This recipe is all about the nostalgia of that delicious cookie dough without any of the risk.

Press-In Chocolate Tart Dough (page 50)

COOKIE DOUGH FILLING

1 cup (115 g) cake flour

10 tablespoons (141 g) salted butter

¾ cup (135 g) brown sugar

1 tablespoon vanilla bean paste

1½ cups (260 g) mini chocolate chips

CHOCOLATE FILLING

7 ounces (198 g) semisweet chocolate, finely chopped

1 cup heavy cream

¼ cup maple syrup

2 teaspoons vanilla bean paste

TO GARNISH

Cream Cheese Whipped Cream (page 277)

Chocolate Fudge Sauce (page 288)

To make the crust: Preheat oven to 350°F. Press tart dough into a 10-inch tart pan. Generously dock with a fork and bake for 25 to 30 minutes or until crust appears dry. While still hot, use a tamper or the back of a spoon to lightly press down the center of the crust, leaving a ¾-inch border around the edge.

To make the flour safe to eat, spread it evenly on a baking sheet and bake for 5 to 6 minutes, stirring once in the middle of the bake time. Allow to cool, and then sift into a medium bowl.

To make the cookie dough: In the bowl of a stand mixer fitted with the paddle attachment, combine butter, sugar, and vanilla bean paste. Mix on medium speed until light and fluffy, about 5 minutes. Add cooled flour and chocolate chips and mix just until combined. Using a rubber spatula, scrape the sides and bottom of the bowl to ensure even mixing. Spread about ¾ of the cookie dough in the cooled tart crust. Cover and refrigerate while making the chocolate filling. Form small balls with the remaining dough (about ¾-inch in diameter). Place in an airtight container and store in the refrigerator until ready to serve.

To make the chocolate filling: Add chopped chocolate to the bowl of a stand mixer fitted with the whisk attachment. In a saucepan, whisk together heavy cream, maple syrup, and vanilla bean paste. Cook over medium-high heat until the mixture is steaming but not boiling. Pour over the chocolate and allow it to sit for 2 minutes. Mix on lowest speed until the chocolate is fully melted and incorporated into the cream mixture. Increase the speed to medium for 1 minute and then beat on high for 5 minutes. Pour over the cookie dough layer. Cover and refrigerate for at least 2 hours before removing from the tart pan. Serve topped with Cream Cheese Whipped Cream, mini cookie dough balls, and drizzles of Chocolate Fudge Sauce.

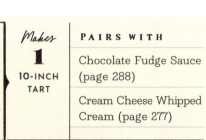

WINTER

Makes
1
10-INCH
TART

PAIRS WITH

Chocolate Fudge Sauce (page 288)

Cream Cheese Whipped Cream (page 277)

Peanut Butter Cup Pie

I have always loved peanut butter pie in all its many forms and iterations. If I spot one on a menu, I will always want to try it. The Peanut Butter Silk Pie (page 197) is one of my long-standing favorites, but this version, inspired by peanut butter cup candy, is also amazing. It's like a cross between homemade peanut butter bars and a chocolate pie. Topped with Whipped Cream, this makes a rich and pretty pie that's certain to be a hit.

Preheat oven to 350°F. Press crust into a deep-dish pie plate and bake for 6 minutes. Allow to cool.

To make the peanut butter layer: Add peanut butter, butter, brown sugar, and vanilla extract to the bowl of a stand mixer fitted with the paddle attachment. Beat on medium speed for 3 to 4 minutes, stopping in the middle to scrape the sides and bottom of the bowl. Add confectioners' sugar 1 cup at a time and mix just until combined. Spread into the cooled pie crust.

To make the chocolate layer: Place chopped chocolate in a heatproof bowl. Place a fine mesh sieve over the bowl and set aside. Whisk together egg, egg yolks, and sugar in a medium saucepan. Cook over medium-high heat, stirring constantly, until mixture becomes thick and coats the back of the spoon, 8 to 10 minutes. Use an instant read thermometer to check the temperature; it should reach 170°F. Pour hot mixture into the sieve directly onto chocolate. Press mixture through the sieve. Allow hot mixture to sit on chocolate for about 1 minute and then stir with a rubber spatula until chocolate has melted and is completely incorporated. Allow the mixture to cool for a few more minutes until it is only warm.

In the bowl of a stand mixer fitted with the paddle attachment, beat butter, vanilla extract, and salt on high until light and fluffy, about 5 minutes. Add cooled chocolate mixture and beat on high for 5 more minutes. Stop once to scrape down the sides and bottom of the bowl to ensure even mixing.

In the bowl of a stand mixer fitted with the whisk attachment, add heavy cream and confectioners' sugar. Beat on high until stiff peaks form, about 4 to 5 minutes. Fold whipped cream gently into cooled chocolate mixture with a rubber spatula. Spread evenly on top of the peanut butter layer. Cover pie and refrigerate for at least 3 hours. Before serving, garnish with Whipped Cream, chopped peanut butter cups, and Chocolate Fudge Sauce.

Deep-Dish Chocolate Wafer Crumb Crust (page 52)

PEANUT BUTTER LAYER
1½ cups (375 g) peanut butter

6 tablespoons (84 g) salted butter, softened

¼ cup (45 g) brown sugar

2 teaspoons vanilla extract

2 cups (220 g) confectioners' sugar

CHOCOLATE LAYER
6 ounces (170 g) dark chocolate, chopped

1 egg

2 egg yolks

¾ cup (150 g) sugar

½ cup (113 g) unsalted butter, softened

2 teaspoons vanilla extract

¼ teaspoon fine sea salt

1 cup heavy cream

3 tablespoons confectioners' sugar

TO GARNISH
Whipped Cream (page 276)

½ cup chopped peanut butter cups

Chocolate Fudge Sauce (page 288), for drizzling

PAIRS WITH

Chocolate Fudge Sauce (page 288)

Whipped Cream (page 276)

Makes
1
DEEP-DISH
PIE

WINTER

Cookies *and* Cream Hand Pies

Two childhood sweet treats combine to make this delightfully sweet hand pie. Black cocoa is the signature ingredient in Oreos, and if you use it in your pie crust you will get more of the flavor that will bring you back to your childhood. With a delicate flaky crust and creamy vanilla filling, this will be a hit with the kids (and the grownups).

Double Black Cocoa Pie Dough (page 35)

FILLING

8 ounces (227 g) cream cheese, softened

½ cup (55 g) confectioners' sugar

2 tablespoons cornstarch

2 teaspoons vanilla extract

3–4 Chocolate Wafer Cookies (page 280) or Oreos, crushed

Egg Wash (page 275)

ICING

2 tablespoons half and half

1 teaspoon vanilla bean paste

1⅓ cups (146 g) confectioners' sugar

TO GARNISH

3–4 Chocolate Wafer Cookies (page 280) or Oreos, crushed

Preheat oven to 375°F and line two baking sheets with parchment paper or silicone baking mats and set aside.

On a lightly floured surface, roll out the first disk of pie dough to about ⅛-inch thick. With a knife or bench scraper, cut out 4½ x 3¼-inch rectangles. Cut as many rectangles as you can, then gather the scraps and roll out dough two more times to get as many rectangles as possible. Repeat with the second disk of dough. You should have 18 rectangles total. Store covered in the refrigerator while you make the filling.

Add cream cheese, confectioners' sugar, cornstarch, and vanilla extract to the bowl of a stand mixer fitted with the paddle attachment. Beat on medium speed for 3 to 4 minutes, stopping in the middle to scrape the bottom and sides of the bowl to ensure even mixing. Stir in the crushed cookies by hand.

Place one dough rectangle on a prepared baking sheet. Add about 4 teaspoons of filling to the center of the rectangle. Spread filling, leaving a ½-inch border. Brush Egg Wash on the border. Cover with a second dough rectangle. With the tines of a fork, crimp edges of pastry and poke a few holes in the top. Repeat with remaining dough rectangles, spacing them out over both baking sheets. Brush tops with Egg Wash. Store one sheet in the refrigerator while the other batch bakes for 22 to 25 minutes. Transfer to a cooling rack and allow to cool completely.

To make the icing: In a medium bowl, whisk together half and half, vanilla bean paste, and confectioners' sugar just until incorporated. With an offset spatula, spread onto tops of cooled pastries. Garnish with crushed Chocolate Wafers or Oreos and serve immediately. Store leftovers in an airtight container for up to 3 days or freeze for up to 2 months.

WINTER

Makes

9

page
248

Chocolate Tart

This tart encapsulates my love of richly delicious desserts. The slightly crisp shortbread crust and smooth decadent filling make the ultimate chocolate combination. It pairs delightfully with a sweet, slightly tart Raspberry Sauce or Salted Caramel. This one is so intense, you'll only need a small piece.

To make the crust: Preheat oven to 350°F. Press tart dough into a 10-inch tart pan. Generously dock with a fork and parbake for 10 minutes. While still hot, use a tamper or the back of a spoon to lightly press down the center of the crust, leaving a ¾-inch edge.

To make the filling: In the bowl of a stand mixer fitted with the whisk attachment, beat eggs, sugar, vanilla, and salt on low for 5 minutes.

In a medium saucepan over medium-high heat, heat heavy cream until it is steaming but not boiling. Remove from heat and add chocolate. Stir until chocolate has melted completely and is fully incorporated. With the mixer running on low, carefully pour the chocolate mixture into the egg mixture. Mix for an additional 3 to 5 minutes until fully incorporated and smooth.

Pour filling into the crust and return to the oven. Bake 15 to 20 minutes or until filling has started to set but is still a little bit jiggly. Allow tart to cool for 20 minutes or longer before removing sides of the pan. Serve with Salted Caramel or Raspberry Sauce and Whipped Cream.

Press-In Chocolate Tart Dough (page 50)

2 eggs

⅓ cup (66 g) sugar

2 teaspoons vanilla extract

½ teaspoon fine sea salt

1 cup heavy cream

7 ounces (198 g) semisweet chocolate, coarsely chopped

TO GARNISH

crust cutouts

fresh fruit

Whipped Cream (page 276)

sprinkles

PAIRS WITH

Raspberry Sauce (page 286)

Salted Caramel (page 289)

Makes **1** 10-INCH ROUND TART

WINTER

Raspberry Cream Pie

This creamy icebox pie is a classically delicious pairing of chocolate and raspberries and will be a hit at any holiday gathering. This is a great make-ahead pie to take the stress from trying to make a dessert last-minute, and the colors are perfect for Christmas.

Deep-Dish Chocolate Wafer Crumb Crust (page 52)

FILLING

12 ounces (340 g) cold cream cheese

1½ cups heavy cream

¾ cup (83 g) confectioners' sugar

2 teaspoons vanilla extract

1¼ cups Raspberry Jam (page 286), divided

GANACHE

3 ounces (85 g) semisweet chocolate, chopped

½ cup heavy cream

TO GARNISH

Milk Chocolate Curls (page 293)

½ cup (63 g) fresh raspberries

6 fresh mint leaves

Preheat oven to 350°F. Press crust into a deep-dish pie plate and bake for 6 minutes. Allow to cool.

To make the filling: In the bowl of a stand mixer fitted with the whisk attachment, beat cream cheese until fluffy, about 4 minutes. Add heavy cream, confectioners' sugar, and vanilla extract, and beat on high until stiff peaks form. Remove from the stand mixer and fold in 2 tablespoons Raspberry Jam with a rubber spatula, taking care not to deflate whipped cream.

Add cream cheese mixture to the bottom of the cooled crust. Top with the remaining jam. Cover and refrigerate while making the ganache.

To make the ganache: Add chopped chocolate to a heatproof bowl. In a small saucepan, cook heavy cream over medium-high heat until steaming but not boiling. Remove from heat. Pour cream over chocolate and allow to sit for about 1 minute. Using a rubber spatula, stir until chocolate is melted and fully incorporated. Allow ganache to sit for 5 to 10 minutes, until it thickens a little, then pour over cooled pie filling. Refrigerate for at least 2 hours before serving. Garnish pie with Milk Chocolate Curls, fresh raspberries, and fresh mint leaves just before serving.

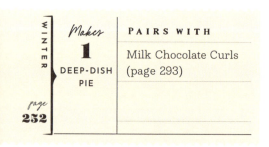

WINTER

Makes

1

DEEP-DISH PIE

PAIRS WITH

Milk Chocolate Curls (page 293)

Red Velvet Pie

One of the best things about working in New York City was the many bakeries one could easily pop into and come out with a perfect cupcake. Red velvet cupcakes were my absolute favorite. This pie version of the popular cake is just as satisfying and delicious. An excellent recipe to bring out for Valentine's Day, this pie topped with Cream Cheese Whipped Cream will bring joy to whomever you serve it.

Preheat oven to 350°F.

Roll out dough on a lightly floured surface to roughly a 15-inch round. Wrap loosely around the rolling pin and transfer to a deep-dish pie plate. Cut off any extra crust and crimp edges.

In the bowl of a stand mixer fitted with the paddle attachment, beat together butter and sugar until light and fluffy, 2 to 3 minutes. Add eggs, vanilla, vinegar, and food coloring. Mix on medium speed until fully incorporated, stopping to scrape sides and bottom of the bowl. In a medium bowl, whisk together flour, salt, and cocoa. Add to butter mixture and mix just until combined.

Pour into the prepared crust and bake for 50 to 60 minutes or until the center is only slightly jiggly. Allow to cool completely before topping with Cream Cheese Whipped Cream. Serve immediately or store in the refrigerator until ready to serve.

Single Butter Pie Dough (page 33)

1 cup (225 g) butter, softened

1⅓ cups (266 g) sugar

3 eggs, room temperature

1 tablespoon vanilla extract

1 teaspoon white distilled vinegar

8 to 10 drops red gel food coloring

¾ cup (98 g) all-purpose flour

½ teaspoon fine sea salt

2 tablespoons unsweetened cocoa powder

Cream Cheese Whipped Cream (page 277)

PAIRS WITH

Cream Cheese Whipped Cream (page 277)

Makes
1
DEEP-DISH PIE

WINTER

Raspberry Cheesecake Valentine Tart

Perfect for Valentine's Day, this cheesecake tart has easy to make raspberry hearts on the top, making this a great gift for your sweetheart or a festive fun tart to share at the office or with friends.

Press-In Chocolate Tart Dough (page 50)

CHEESECAKE FILLING

8 ounces (227 g) cream cheese, softened

1 tablespoon unsalted butter, softened

⅓ cup (66 g) sugar

1 egg

2 tablespoons buttermilk

1 tablespoon all-purpose flour

1 teaspoon vanilla extract

⅓ cup Raspberry Sauce (page 287)

To make the crust: Preheat oven to 350°F. Press tart dough into a 10-inch tart pan. Generously dock with a fork and parbake for 15 minutes. While still hot, use a tamper or the back of a spoon to lightly press down the center of the crust, leaving a ¾-inch border around the edge.

In the bowl of a stand mixer fitted with the paddle attachment, beat cream cheese, butter, and sugar until light and fluffy, about 5 minutes. Add egg, buttermilk, flour, and vanilla extract and beat until fully combined and smooth. Scrape the bottom and sides of the bowl with a rubber spatula to ensure even mixing. Pour into the prepared crust.

Add small circles of Raspberry Sauce to the top of the cheesecake filling. Drag a toothpick or skewer from top to bottom through each raspberry circle to create heart shapes. Bake for 30 to 35 minutes or until edges are set and the center still jiggles a little. Cool completely and then cover and refrigerate for at least 4 hours.

Remove tart from the pan and serve garnished with more Raspberry Sauce and White Chocolate Curls.

Makes
1
10-INCH TART

PAIRS WITH

White Chocolate Curls (page 293)

Raspberry Sauce (page 287)

Raspberry Heart Hand Pies

Adorable and sweet, these little cream cheese and raspberry hand pies are great any time of the year but are especially fun for Valentine's Day. Making the cutouts and assembling them is a fun activity to get kids involved in.

two baking sheets with parchment paper or silicone baking mats and set aside.

On a lightly floured surface, roll out the first disk of pie dough to about ⅛-inch thick. With a 4- or 5-inch heart-shaped cookie cutter, cut out as many hearts as you can and then gather the scraps and roll out dough two more times to get as many hearts as possible. Repeat with the second disk of dough. You should have about 30 hearts total.

To make the filling: In the bowl of a stand mixer fitted with the paddle attachment, beat cream cheese, sugar, and vanilla extract on medium speed until smooth.

To assemble: Place the first 2 dough hearts on a prepared baking sheet. Brush both hearts with Egg Wash. Add about 1 tablespoon cream cheese mixture to the center of 1 heart and spread a little, leaving a ½-inch border. Top with about 1 tablespoon jam. Place the second dough heart over the filling, Egg Wash–side down. With the tines of a fork, crimp edges of pastry and poke a few holes in the top crust. Repeat with remaining dough hearts, spacing them out over both baking sheets. Brush tops with Egg Wash. Refrigerate for 20 minutes before baking. Bake one sheet at a time for 17 to 20 minutes or until golden brown on top. Transfer to a cooling rack and allow to cool completely.

To make the glaze: In a small bowl, whisk together all ingredients except sprinkles until thoroughly combined. Brush tops and sides of cooled pies with icing, then top with sprinkles, if using, and serve immediately. Store leftovers in an airtight container for up to 3 days or freeze for up to 2 months.

Double Butter Pie Dough (page 33)

FILLING

6 ounces (170 g) cream cheese, softened

½ cup (100 g) sugar

1 teaspoon vanilla extract

½ cup Raspberry Jam (page 286)

Egg Wash (page 275)

GLAZE

3 tablespoons half and half

1 teaspoon vanilla extract

1½ cups (165 g) confectioners' sugar

3 drops pink or red gel food coloring

sprinkles, optional

Preheat oven to 400°F and line

Makes about **15**

WINTER

Valentine Almond Berry Pie

The almond filling in this pie is based on the filling for banket, a popular Dutch dessert from the community where I grew up. The almond filling is delicious with the berries. Top the whole thing with a heart-themed top crust for a lovely Valentine pie.

Double Butter Pie Dough (page 33)

BERRY FILLING

¾ cup (150 g) sugar

2 tablespoons cornstarch

½ teaspoon fine sea salt

1 cup (125 g) fresh raspberries

¾ cup (138 g) chopped strawberries

¾ cup (148 g) blueberries

1 teaspoon vanilla extract

1 tablespoon unsalted butter

ALMOND FILLING

8 ounces (227 g) almond paste

1 egg

1 cup (200 g) sugar

½ teaspoon almond extract

Egg Wash (page 275)

To make the berry filling: In a medium bowl, whisk together sugar, cornstarch, and salt. In a medium saucepan, add berries, vanilla, and butter. Cook over medium heat until berries start to break down. Add sugar mixture and cook for an additional 3 to 4 minutes until slightly thickened. It will thicken more while baking. Remove from heat and cool to room temperature.

To make the crust: Preheat oven to 400°F. Roll out the first disk of pie dough on a lightly floured surface to roughly a 15-inch round. Wrap loosely around the rolling pin and transfer to a deep-dish pie plate. Cut off any extra crust and crimp edges.

To make the almond filling: In the bowl of a stand mixer fitted with the paddle attachment, add almond paste, egg, sugar, and almond extract. Beat until smooth and fully combined. Pour into prepared crust. Pour berry filling over the almond layer.

Roll out the second disk of dough on a lightly floured surface. Using a heart-shaped cookie cutter, create cutouts and add them to the top of the pie. Brush the cutouts with Egg Wash. Place pie on a rimmed baking sheet to catch any drips and bake for about 50 to 60 minutes or until crust is golden brown and filling is bubbling. Allow to cool for 20 minutes before cutting. Serve warm with Vanilla Bean Ice Cream.

WINTER

Makes

1

DEEP-DISH PIE

G✳F

PAIRS WITH

Vanilla Bean Ice Cream (page 279)

Mediterranean Quiche

I like to make this quiche in the dark days of winter to remind me of the sun-drenched Mediterranean and to look forward to longer, brighter days. The ingredients are readily available year-round, and the flavors will bring comfort any day of the year. It also makes a great vegetarian dish to add to a spread for a party or gathering.

Parbake the crust in a deep-dish pie plate according to the instructions on page 41. Reduce oven temperature to 375°F.

To make the filling: In the bowl of a stand mixer fitted with the whisk attachment, beat milk and cream on medium speed for 3 minutes. Add eggs and beat for an additional 2 minutes. Add black pepper and oregano; mix until combined. Set aside.

In a medium bowl, combine tomatoes, scallions, olives, and feta and transfer to the parbaked crust. Pour egg mixture over vegetables.

Set quiche on a rimmed baking sheet and loosely cover with foil. Bake for 30 minutes, remove foil, and bake for an additional 30 minutes or until the top of the quiche is golden brown and a cake tester inserted in the middle comes out clean. Garnish with cilantro and serve immediately.

✽ *The ingredients in this quiche have plenty of salt, so be sure not to add any to the egg mixture.*

✽ *Most kalamata olives are gluten-free (preserved in red wine vinegar) but some are not (preserved in malt vinegar). Check your olives carefully if your quiche needs to be gluten-free.*

Single Butter Pie Dough (page 33)

FILLING

¾ cup whole milk

¾ cup heavy cream

4 eggs

½ teaspoon black pepper

½ teaspoon dried oregano

¾ cup (125 g) chopped tomatoes

½ cup (25 g) sliced scallions

⅓ cup (60 g) pitted and sliced kalamata olives

1½ cups (180 g) crumbled feta cheese

OPTIONAL GARNISH

⅓ cup chopped fresh cilantro

Makes **1** DEEP-DISH PIE

WINTER

GF

page **263**

Potato, Bacon, *and* Gruyère Galette

It might sound like too much to take richly cheesy potatoes and add them to a delicate buttery crust, but trust me, you won't regret the excess when you try a slice of this galette. The gruyère and bacon give amazing flavor, and the neat crust package makes a beautiful presentation.

Single Butter Pie Dough (page 33)

1 pound (454 g) potatoes, peeled

1 pound (454 g) bacon

CHEESE SAUCE

3 scallions

1 tablespoon salted butter

⅓ cup heavy cream

3 tablespoons all-purpose flour

⅔ cup whole milk

2½ ounces (71 g) gruyère, shredded

fine sea salt and pepper, to taste

Egg Wash (page 275)

TO GARNISH

2 ounces (57 g) gruyère, shredded

¼ cup reserved bacon

sliced scallion greens

Slice potatoes with a mandoline or a food processor set to the thinnest slice, or slice potatoes as thinly as you can by hand. Add potato slices to a bowl of cold water to prevent browning. Set aside.

Cook bacon in a skillet or nonstick pan over medium heat until crisp. Turn frequently to avoid burning. Place bacon on plate lined with paper towel. Drain grease and wipe out the skillet.

Slice scallions, reserving green portions to garnish. Melt butter in the same skillet that bacon was cooked in and add white scallion slices. Cook over medium heat for about 4 minutes. Add heavy cream and cook for an additional 2 minutes. Sprinkle flour over mixture and whisk until a paste forms. Add milk and continue whisking until smooth. Add cheese and whisk until fully melted and incorporated. Add salt and pepper to taste. Cook for 2 minutes more, until bubbly and thickened. Remove from heat.

Finely chop the cooled bacon. Reserve ¼ cup to garnish and mix the rest into the cheese sauce. Drain potato slices and add to cheese sauce, stirring gently to coat.

Preheat oven to 375°F. Line a half-sheet pan with parchment paper. Roll out pie dough into a 15-inch round. Wrap loosely around rolling pin and transfer to center of prepared pan. Place filling on crust, leaving a 2- to 3-inch border. Arrange potato slices in neat layers, checking that each slice is coated in cheese sauce. Fold edges of crust up and over, partially overlapping the filling. Pinch crust where it overlaps itself to seal in the filling and prevent leaks. Brush Egg Wash on top crust. Loosely cover with a sheet of foil and bake for 25 minutes, then remove foil and bake for an additional 20 minutes. Pull oven rack out and carefully sprinkle shredded gruyère on top of potatoes. Bake for an additional 15 minutes or until crust is golden brown and cheese is bubbling and lightly browned. Sprinkle galette with reserved scallions and bacon. Cut and serve immediately.

Sausage Ricotta Pie

When I was a kid, trips to Chicago usually meant getting the eponymous deep-dish pizza. This sausage and ricotta stuffed savory pie is inspired by the great pies of the Windy City but made with pie crust instead of a yeast-based dough. This amazingly comforting and piping-hot pie disappears in short order when served to family and friends.

Preheat oven to 400°F. Roll out first disk of dough on a lightly floured surface to roughly a 15-inch round. Wrap loosely around the rolling pin and transfer to a deep-dish pie plate. Press into the dish so the dough comes in contact with the entire pan. Leave extra crust on edges.

Brown sausage and drain any fat. In a medium bowl, mix together ricotta and Romano cheeses. Add sausage, grape tomatoes, and mozzarella pearls. Chiffonade basil leaves and add. Mix until fully combined. Pour into prepared pie crust and smooth evenly. Brush dough edges with Egg Wash.

On a lightly floured surface, roll out second disk of pie dough. Lay on top of pie. Pinch the top and bottom crust edges together. Cut off any crust that extends more than 2 inches over the edge of the pan. Roll and crimp crust. Brush the entire top of the pie with Egg Wash. With a sharp knife, make several vents in the top crust.

Loosely cover with foil and bake for 30 minutes. Remove the foil and bake for an additional 20 to 25 minutes or until the top is golden brown.

Warm marinara sauce in a saucepan over medium heat. Spoon onto top crust and sprinkle with Parmesan. (Or serve sauce on the side.) Garnish with fresh basil and serve immediately.

Double Butter Pie Dough (page 33)

FILLING

1 pound (454 g) ground sausage

16 ounces (464 g) whole milk ricotta cheese

1 ounce (28 g) Romano cheese, shredded

⅔ cup (128 g) grape tomatoes, sliced

8 ounces (227 g) fresh mozzarella pearls, drained

12 fresh basil leaves, plus more to garnish

Egg Wash (page 275)

TOPPING

2 cups high-quality marinara sauce

½ cup (45 g) shredded Parmesan

Makes

1

DEEP-DISH PIE

G✳F

WINTER

page **267**

Cranberry Brie Skillet Galette

This galette makes a fabulous centerpiece for a holiday appetizer spread or large charcuterie board. It's perfect for either Thanksgiving or Christmas or any of the many December gatherings that make this time of year so much fun. The sweet, tart, and savory filling goes great with the crust and with crackers and baguette slices, and it will be a beautiful part of your table spread.

1½ Butter Pie Dough (page 33)

CRANBERRY SAUCE

⅓ cup (66 g) sugar

1 tablespoon cornstarch

⅛ teaspoon fine sea salt

¼ teaspoon cinnamon

3 cups (300 g) fresh cranberries

1 tablespoon fresh lemon juice

⅓ cup orange juice

⅓ cup honey

8 ounces (227 g) Brie (one wheel)

Egg Wash (page 275)

½ cup (53 g) finely chopped pecans

2 sprigs fresh rosemary, to garnish

Preheat oven to 400°F.

To make the cranberry sauce: In a small bowl, whisk together sugar, cornstarch, salt, and cinnamon. In the bowl of a food processor, process cranberries until finely chopped. Add sugar mixture and pulse to combine. In a medium saucepan, add lemon juice, orange juice, honey, and cranberry mixture. Bring to a boil over medium-high heat. Continue cooking, stirring frequently, until most of the cranberries have broken down and juices have thickened, about 10 minutes.

Roll out dough on a lightly floured surface to roughly an 18-inch round. Wrap loosely around the rolling pin and transfer to a 12-inch skillet. Allow extra crust to drape over the edges of the skillet.

To assemble: Cut the rind from the top of the Brie wheel, then cut the wheel into 8 wedges. Place Brie on the crust in the shape of a circle but with about ½ inch of space between each wedge. Top with about ⅔ of the cranberry sauce. Fold edges of crust up and over, partially overlapping the filling. Brush top crust with Egg Wash and sprinkle the entire galette with pecans.

Bake for 25 to 30 minutes or until top crust is golden brown and filling is bubbling. Garnish with fresh rosemary and serve warm with crackers, Toffee Pecans, and the extra cranberry sauce.

WINTER

Makes
1
12-INCH SKILLET GALETTE

G✳F

PAIRS WITH

Toffee Pecans
(page 290)

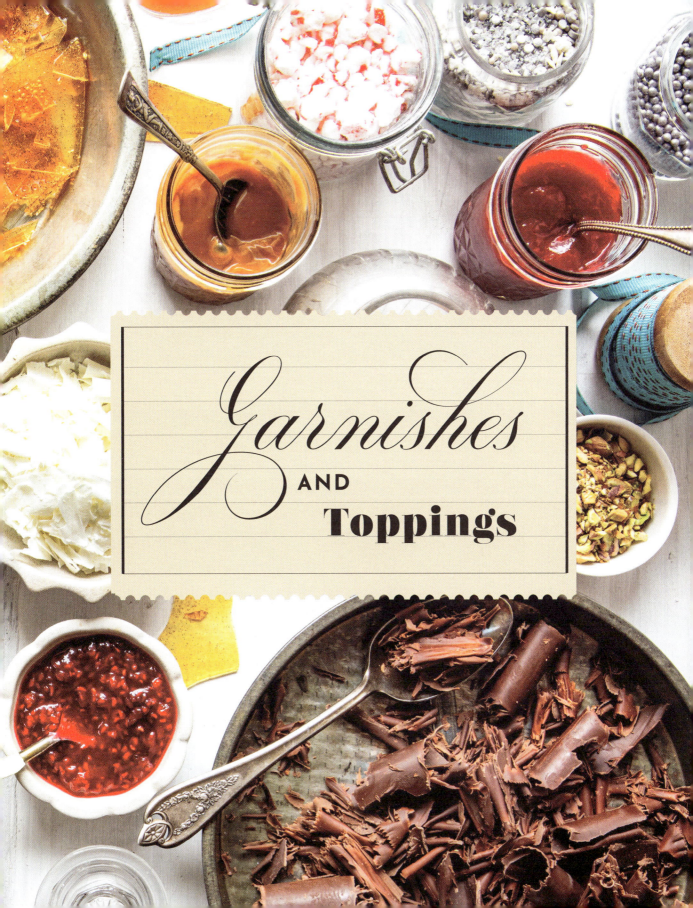

Garnishes
AND
Toppings

Garnishing Pies and Tarts

There are many ways to make the delicious pies, tarts, and galettes in this book even more decadent, as well as more beautiful. Because many of these packages of dessert joy are perfect to serve at holidays, celebrations, and gatherings—or to give as gifts—a little extra care to make them more festive is sometimes in order. Here are some ideas to decorate your baked treats as well as some recipes that make perfect accompaniments for them.

DECORATED TARTS

The top of a tart is sometimes like a blank canvas, just begging to be ornamented. Some of my favorite things to use to make tarts into mini edible works of art are listed below. I like to arrange toppings around the edges, leaving the center plain so you can still see the tart filling. A crescent shape of ornamental toppings on just one side of the tart is also beautiful.

Seasonal Candy and Sprinkles

Craft stores, grocery stores, and big-box stores frequently have seasonal candy and baking supplies that can easily bring holiday and seasonal charm to your tarts. Sprinkles can instantly make your dessert look more festive, perfect for a birthday or New Year's celebration. Treats like mini chocolate eggs, shamrock candies, and chocolate stars are also fun toppers to use.

Fresh and Sugared Fruit

Sliced fruit and berries are a beautiful way to add color to the top of a summer tart. Sugared fruit such as Sugared Cranberries are extra elegant and especially nice on Christmas tarts.

Fresh Edible Flowers and Herbs

Small flowers interspersed with other ornamental toppings make beautiful tarts, especially for a Mother's Day celebration or wedding shower. Fresh herbs are an excellent way to add some green to the canvas. Rosemary sprigs have an evergreen look, making them a lovely addition to Christmas tarts. Fresh mint leaves look great with fresh fruit on summer and spring tarts.

Homemade Cookies and Pie Cutouts

Miniature cookies, Chocolate Wafers, and small pie crust cutouts are a fun way to add more homemade deliciousness to your tarts. Pie crust cookie cutters and cookie stamps are excellent for customizing treats and a great way to get kids involved in baking.

DECORATED PIES AND GALETTES

Piped Whipped Cream

Piping on Whipped Cream with a large star tip will always make a pie a little more special. You can try a variety of piping methods, from creating a simple border around the edge of the pie to creating a pattern of swirls, stars, and lines across the entire top of the pie.

Drizzled Sauces

A drizzle of Salted Caramel or honey over a rustic galette will add more visual interest as well as more flavor. Chocolate and fruit sauces are pretty drizzled over piped Whipped Cream. For more control on how you drizzle, put your sauce in a disposable pastry bag or resealable plastic bag, trim off the tip of the bag to create a small opening, and drizzle over the pie or galette just before serving.

Crunchy Decorative Toppings

Toffee Pecans, Caramel Shards, and crushed cookies add texture and crunch to your finished pie. They look nice sprinkled on Whipped Cream or Vanilla Bean Ice Cream. You can also serve these homemade treats on the side so guests can customize their pie.

Egg Wash *and* Sweet Egg Wash

Using Egg Wash on top crusts and galettes will give your finished baked goods a more golden look and a little shine. It's worth the extra step for the beautiful appearance and slight crispness. Use without the optional sugar for savory pies, and add the sugar if desired for sweet pies.

In a medium bowl, whisk egg and water until slightly foamy and fully incorporated. There should be no patches of egg white or yolk visible. Add sugar if Sweet Egg Wash is desired and whisk until fully incorporated. Using a pastry brush, fully cover the top crust before baking. Store leftovers in an airtight container for up to 2 days. Whisk again before using leftover Egg Wash.

1 egg

1 tablespoon cold water

1 tablespoon sugar, optional

Whipped Cream

Makes about **4** CUPS

Real Whipped Cream is the perfect topping for sweet pies. It is the most popular pie accompaniment at our house, and this generously scaled recipe will ensure there is enough to go around.

2 cups heavy cream

⅓ cup (36 g) confectioners' sugar

2 teaspoons vanilla extract or vanilla bean paste

In the bowl of a stand mixer fitted with the whisk attachment, add heavy cream. Beat on medium speed until it starts to thicken. Stop the mixer and add the confectioners' sugar and vanilla. Beat on high until medium peaks form.

Pile the Whipped Cream on top of a pie, add it to a large pastry bag with a large star tip and pipe it onto a pie, or serve on the side and allow guests to dollop on as much as they want.

✱ *Homemade Whipped Cream will deflate over time. For best results, make it just before serving. Always keep leftover pie with Whipped Cream topping stored in the refrigerator.*

Cream Cheese Whipped Cream

Makes about **3** CUPS

This rich, more dense variation is incredibly delicious and more stable than plain Whipped Cream. It is excellent for piping on top of cooled pies and pairs nicely with most sweet pies. I especially love this on Red Velvet Pie (page 204), Pumpkin Cheesecake Pie (page 255), and Fresh Strawberry Icebox Pie (page 111). Give it a try on your pies and desserts; you can swap this one in for any pie that normally goes great with regular Whipped Cream.

In the bowl of a stand mixer fitted with the whisk attachment, beat cream cheese, vanilla extract, and confectioners' sugar on medium speed until light, fluffy, and smooth, about 5 minutes. With the mixer running on low, slowly add heavy cream. Once cream is incorporated, increase the speed to high. Continue beating until stiff peaks form, about 5 minutes.

Either pile on top of your pie, pipe onto your pie with a large star tip, or serve on the side and allow guests to add as much as they want.

✽ *For best results, make just before serving. Always keep leftover pie with Cream Cheese Whipped Cream topping stored in the refrigerator.*

6 ounces (170 g) cold cream cheese

2 teaspoons vanilla extract (or vanilla bean paste)

¾ cup (83 g) confectioners' sugar

1½ cups heavy cream, cold

Vanilla Bean Ice Cream

Makes **1** QUART

The phrase "pie à la mode" has been used for over a century, demonstrating just how popular adding a scoop of vanilla ice cream to pie has been and continues to be. And what could be better than homemade vanilla ice cream made with fragrant vanilla bean seeds? Make this a day in advance of your pie to give the ice cream time to fully freeze. Serve over warm pie for a delicious dessert.

In a small bowl, combine ¼ cup milk with cornstarch and mix until all lumps have dissolved. In a medium pot over medium heat, add remaining milk and heavy cream, then whisk in the cornstarch slurry. Add sugar and malted milk powder and whisk to combine. On a cutting board, cut vanilla bean lengthwise with a sharp knife. Scrape the seeds from the inside of the vanilla bean and add to the milk mixture. Stir until vanilla bean seeds are distributed. Continue cooking over medium-high heat, stirring frequently, until the mixture just about reaches a boil. Reduce heat to medium-low and continue cooking until cream mixture thickens, about 5 more minutes. Allow to cool, then cover and chill in the refrigerator for at least 2 hours or overnight.

Add chilled cream mixture to the ice cream maker and follow manufacturer's instructions to churn into ice cream. When ice cream is finished, scoop into an airtight container. Cover and freeze for at least 2 hours or overnight. Serve with your favorite pie.

❋ *Malted milk powder is typically not gluten-free. To guarantee your sweet and creamy treat is gluten-free, check your ingredients carefully or follow the vanilla ice cream recipe variation on page 128.*

2 cups whole milk, divided

2 tablespoons cornstarch

2 cups heavy cream

¾ cup (150 g) sugar

¼ cup (35 g) malted milk powder

1 vanilla bean (or 1 tablespoon vanilla bean paste)

Chocolate Wafer Cookies

Chocolate Wafer Cookies are the basis of delicious crumb crusts. You can use storebought if you're in a rush, but this recipe will give you the chance to create a totally homemade pie. These cookies also make great ornamental toppers when propped in Whipped Cream or laid on top of tarts. They hold their shape nicely, making this a perfect recipe for using an embossed rolling pin or cookie stamp for added texture.

1 cup (225 g) unsalted butter, softened

1 cup (200 g) sugar

1 egg, room temperature

1 teaspoon vanilla extract

¼ cup corn syrup

2 cups (260 g) all-purpose flour

½ teaspoon baking soda

½ teaspoon fine sea salt

¾ cup (75 g) black cocoa powder

Preheat oven to 350°F. Line a baking sheet with parchment paper or a silicone baking mat.

In the bowl of a stand mixer fitted with the paddle attachment, beat butter, sugar, egg, vanilla, and corn syrup until light and fluffy, about 5 minutes. In a medium bowl, combine flour, baking soda, and salt. Sift cocoa into the flour mixture. Add to the butter mixture and beat just until combined. Divide dough in half. On a floured surface, roll out one portion until it is about ¼- inch thick. Make cutouts with a 1-inch round cookie cutter. Roll out the scraps to make as many wafers as possible. Repeat with the second portion of dough. Transfer cutouts to the cookie sheet, leaving about an inch of space between cookies. Bake for 10 to 12 minutes or until wafers look dry. Allow cookies to cool on the sheet for 5 minutes before transferring to a cooling rack. After cookies have cooled completely, store in an airtight container for up to 3 days or in the freezer for up to 3 months.

Vanilla Wafer Cookies

Makes about **80**

These little Vanilla Wafer cookies are so much better than the storebought variety. Using pure vanilla bean paste instead of artificial flavors really makes a difference. They can be served with puddings, ground to make a crumb crust, or eaten on their own.

1 cup (225 g) unsalted butter, softened

1 cup (200 g) sugar

2 eggs

1 tablespoon vanilla bean paste

2½ cups (325 g) all-purpose flour

½ teaspoon fine sea salt

2 teaspoons baking powder

Preheat oven to 350°F. Line a baking sheet with parchment paper or a silicone baking mat.

In the bowl of a stand mixer fitted with the paddle attachment, beat butter and sugar on medium-high speed until light and fluffy, about 5 minutes. Add eggs and vanilla bean paste and beat until combined.

In a small mixing bowl, combine flour, salt, and baking powder. Add to the butter mixture and beat on medium-low speed just until combined.

Using a ½-ounce cookie scoop, scoop dough onto the prepared baking sheet, leaving 1½ inches of space between each cookie.

Bake just until cookies are golden on edges, about 14 to 16 minutes. Allow cookies to cool on the sheet for about 5 minutes before transferring to a cooling rack. Store in an airtight container for up to 3 days or freeze for up to 3 months.

Oatmeal Cookie Crisps

Makes **48**

This recipe is based on an old chocolate chip cookie recipe my mom used to make when I was growing up. The vegetable oil may seem like an odd ingredient choice, but it yields unique and crisp cookies that are perfect for making crumbs for crust and also taste great on their own.

Preheat oven to 350°F. Line a baking sheet with parchment paper or a silicone baking mat.

In the bowl of a stand mixer fitted with the paddle attachment, beat butter and sugars on medium-high speed until light and fluffy, about 5 minutes. Add oil, eggs, and vanilla and beat until combined.

In a small mixing bowl, combine flour, salt, and baking soda. Add to the butter mixture and beat on medium-low speed just until combined. Remove bowl from mixer and, using a rubber spatula, stir in the oatmeal.

Using a 1-ounce cookie scoop, scoop dough onto the prepared baking sheet, leaving 2 inches of space between each cookie.

Bake just until cookies are light brown across the full top of the cookie, about 16 to 20 minutes. Allow cookies to cool on the sheet for about 5 minutes before transferring them to a cooling rack. Store in an airtight container for up to 3 days or freeze for up to 3 months.

1 cup (225 g) unsalted butter, softened

1 cup (200 g) granulated sugar

1 cup (180 g) brown sugar

1 cup vegetable oil

1 egg

1 tablespoon vanilla extract

3¾ cups (488 g) all-purpose flour

1 teaspoon fine sea salt

1 teaspoon baking soda

2 cups (160 g) old-fashioned oatmeal

Sugared Cranberries

Cranberries are one of the only fruits in season in late fall and early winter, so take advantage of these berries to add a pop of color to your holiday pies. This simple to make recipe will add even more flair to this already pretty fruit.

In a medium saucepan over medium-high heat, combine 1 cup sugar and water to make simple syrup. Bring mixture to a boil over medium-high heat. Continue boiling until sugar is completely dissolved and the mixture becomes clear instead of cloudy. Allow to cool for 10 minutes, then gently stir in cranberries. Cool completely.

Place a cooling rack on a rimmed baking sheet. When completely cool, remove cranberries from the saucepan with a slotted spoon and arrange them on the cooling rack to dry. Separate each cranberry so none are touching each other. Allow cranberries to dry for about 1 hour. You will know they are ready when they stick to your finger.

Pour remaining sugar into a medium bowl. Toss cranberries in the sugar gently to coat, taking care they don't stick to each other. Place them in a bowl to serve or in a single layer in an airtight container to store. Use to garnish your favorite holiday desserts.

✽ *Variation: This same process works on fresh mint leaves, rose petals, and rosemary to create a variety of beautiful, edible garnishes.*

2¼ cups (450 g) sugar, divided

1 cup water

2 cups (200 g) fresh cranberries

Raspberry Jam

Makes **1** PINT

Raspberries are an all-time favorite of mine, and since they taste good year-round, they make a nice addition to many varieties of pies. This jam is handy to have on hand for pie and tart fillings.

1 tablespoon water

1 tablespoon cornstarch

4 cups (500 g) fresh raspberries

1¼ cups (250 g) sugar

2 tablespoons fresh lemon juice

1 teaspoon vanilla extract

In a small bowl or cup, mix cornstarch with water until smooth. In a medium saucepan, combine raspberries, sugar, lemon juice, and cornstarch slurry over medium-high heat. As you stir, the raspberries will break down and turn to liquid. Bring mixture to a boil, then reduce temperature to medium. Cook and stir until mixture thickens and coats the back of the spoon, about 8 to 9 minutes. Keep in mind that the jam will thicken more when it has fully cooled. Remove from heat and stir in the vanilla extract.

Pour into a glass pint jar and store in the refrigerator for up to 2 weeks.

Raspberry *or* Blueberry Sauce

This sauce makes an excellent accompaniment to pies and ice cream. You can use either raspberries or blueberries. The raspberry version is especially good with chocolate, and the blueberry is a nice complement to lemon. Both sauces are amazing on pancakes and waffles.

In a small bowl or cup, mix cornstarch with water until smooth. In a medium saucepan over medium-high heat, combine berries, sugar, lemon juice, and cornstarch slurry. As you stir, the berries will break down and turn to liquid. Bring mixture to a boil, then reduce temperature to medium. Cook and stir until the mixture thickens and coats the back of the spoon, about 8 to 9 minutes.

Strain through a fine mesh sieve into a spouted bowl. Use a rubber spatula to push as much of the sauce through the sieve as possible. Pour into a glass jar and allow to cool completely. Cover and store in the refrigerator for up to 1 week.

1 tablespoon water

1 tablespoon cornstarch

4 cups (500 g) raspberries or blueberries

¾ cup (150 g) sugar

1 teaspoon lemon juice

Chocolate Fudge Sauce

This nostalgic recipe is based on an old recipe from my mother. She used unsweetened baker's chocolate, and it always came out amazing but with tiny lumps. I discovered that using a higher quality semisweet chocolate yields a smoother and even more delicious result. This sauce is so versatile and decadent that I keep my refrigerator stocked with it at all times. My son adores it and uses it frequently on ice cream. It's so popular at our house that it seldom lasts long. Luckily it is so easy to make, I don't have any trouble making a new batch whenever we run out.

1 (12 ounce) can evaporated milk

½ cup (113 g) unsalted butter

¼ teaspoon fine sea salt

6 ounces (170 g) semisweet chocolate, coarsely chopped

1 teaspoon vanilla extract

3 cups (330 g) confectioners' sugar

In a medium saucepan over medium heat, add evaporated milk, butter, and salt. Cook until butter has completely melted. Add chocolate and whisk until fully melted. Add vanilla and whisk to combine. Add confectioners' sugar 1 cup at a time, stirring to fully incorporate before adding the next cup. Increase heat to medium-high and cook until the mixture thickens, stirring constantly, about 3 more minutes. Allow sauce to cool in the saucepan for about 10 minutes and then transfer to two pint jars. Cool completely, then cover and refrigerate.

✿ *To revive Chocolate Fudge Sauce, you can either place in a heatproof bowl and microwave on medium until it becomes fluid and warm, stirring frequently, or warm in a small saucepan over medium heat.*

Salted Caramel

Makes 1½ CUPS

This homemade Salted Caramel pairs with so many pies in this book. It's great to always have a jar handy in the refrigerator.

Fill a small bowl half full with water and set it near the stove with a pastry brush. In a medium Dutch oven or heavy-bottomed pot, add ⅓ cup water and sugar. Whisk together and cook over high heat until sugar starts to melt. Continue cooking without stirring, swirling pan occasionally. If sugar starts to stick to the sides of the pot, brush with a wet pastry brush. Cook until sugar turns a medium amber, about 10 minutes. Time will vary, so be sure to keep a close watch. Sugar can go from caramelized to burned quickly.

Turn off heat. Pour heavy cream in slowly, down the side of the pot. The mixture will bubble and may spatter. Add vanilla bean paste and salt and whisk until fully incorporated. Pour into a glass jar. Allow to cool completely, cover, and refrigerate for up to 3 weeks.

❁ To serve Salted Caramel after refrigerating, scoop the amount needed into a small heatproof bowl and microwave in 15-second intervals—stirring in between—until smooth and warm.

⅓ cup water, plus more for brushing

1¾ (350 g) cups sugar

½ teaspoon fine sea salt

¾ cup heavy cream, room temperature

2 teaspoons vanilla bean paste

Toffee Pecans

These nuts are nice to have on hand to easily add some salty sweet crunch to your treats and are a lovely addition sprinkled on the Whipped Cream of strawberry, cherry, apple, and chocolate pies. They are also delicious on ice cream or pancakes.

2 cups (200 g) unsalted pecan halves (or other nuts)

10 tablespoons (141 g) unsalted butter

1 cup (180 g) brown sugar

½ teaspoon fine sea salt

1 tablespoon water

1 tablespoon vanilla extract

Line a 9 × 13 inch pan with parchment paper. Coarsely chop pecans and spread out evenly in the lined pan. Set pan on a hot pad near the stove.

In a medium saucepan fitted with a candy thermometer, melt butter over medium-high heat. Add brown sugar, salt, water, and vanilla extract and whisk until fully incorporated. Continue to cook while stirring until the mixture reaches 300°F. Immediately pour hot toffee over pecans. Allow to cool completely. Break up pecans by chopping on a cutting board. Store in an airtight container for up to 2 weeks. To serve, sprinkle over pies or add to a dessert spread as an optional garnish for guests.

✤ *Variation: You can swap the pecans with walnuts, peanuts, or almonds.*

Caramel Shards

These fun and delicious candy shards make a gorgeous topper to tarts and pies. I especially love using these amber beauties in the fall to add to the warm jewel tones of the season.

Line a half-sheet baking pan with parchment paper and place on a hot pad near the stove. Set a second sheet of parchment paper and a rolling pin nearby.

Fill a small bowl half full with water and set near the stove with a pastry brush. In a medium Dutch oven or heavy-bottomed saucepan, add sugar and water. On a cutting board with a sharp knife, cut open the vanilla bean lengthwise. With the edge of the knife, scrape the seeds from inside the bean and add to the saucepan. Whisk together sugar, water, and vanilla bean seeds. Cook over high heat until sugar starts to melt. Continue cooking without stirring. If sugar starts to stick to the sides of the pot, brush with a wet pastry brush. Cook until sugar turns a medium amber, about 10 minutes. Time will vary, so be sure to keep a close watch. Sugar can go from caramelized to burned quickly.

Pour caramel onto the prepared baking sheet. Place the second piece of parchment over the caramel and use the rolling pin to roll the caramel into a thin, even layer. Allow caramel to cool completely and then break into pieces. Add to the top of your pie just before serving. Store shards in an airtight container at room temperature. Do not store in the refrigerator—the shards will get sticky if you do.

1 cup (200 g) sugar

3 tablespoons water

1 vanilla bean

Chocolate Curls

I love the way a pile of lovely curled chocolate looks on a Whipped Cream-topped pie. I've never had much success making them directly from a bar of chocolate. They usually come out more like shavings than curls. For this method, you can use either a double boiler or the microwave, and you will get large, beautiful curls–perfect for adding both visual interest and more delicious chocolate to your pies.

Set out a half-sheet baking pan. The bottom of the pan should be flat for best results.

Double boiler method: In a double boiler, heat water to just a simmer in the bottom pan. Water should not touch the top pan. Place chocolate and coconut oil in the top pan, taking care not to spill any water into the chocolate. Stir chocolate with a rubber spatula until melted. Remove the top pan and wipe away any water that may have condensed on its outside with a towel. Pour chocolate onto baking sheet, spread evenly, and allow to set.

Microwave method: Add chocolate and coconut oil to a heatproof bowl. Microwave on 30% power for 1 minute. Stir and return to the microwave at 30% for 30-second intervals until chocolate has fully melted and coconut oil is fully incorporated. Pour chocolate onto baking sheet, spread evenly, and allow to set.

To make the curls: The chocolate needs to be firmly set in order for the curls to come out, but the chocolate will be too cold if it's been refrigerated for 30 minutes or more. Room temperature works great in the winter, but in summer months the chocolate may need to go in the refrigerator for about 10 minutes after it sets at room temperature. Use a flat-edged metal spatula to scrape the chocolate off the pan. You can scrape thin layers from the surface of the chocolate or scrape the full layer of chocolate. The chocolate should curl and break off in a variety of shapes and sizes. Place the curls directly on top of your finished pie or store in an airtight container in the refrigerator until ready to use.

7 ounces (198 g) high-quality chocolate (preferred darkness) or white chocolate

1 teaspoon coconut oil

❈ *When I use these curls with ice cream pies, I increase the coconut oil to 1 tablespoon. The extra oil makes the chocolate softer, which will keep it from becoming rock-hard when frozen.*

Resources

PIE TOOLS AND PANS

ATECO
AtecoUSA.com

SUR LA TABLE
SurLaTable.com

WILLIAMS SONOMA
WilliamsSonoma.com

NORDIC WARE
NordicWare.com

FARM HOUSE POTTERY
FarmHousePottery.com

ANTHROPOLOGIE
Anthropologie.com

FOOD-GRADE GIFT PACKAGING

PAPER MART
PaperMart.com

AMAZON
Amazon.com

CHOCOLATE

VALRHONA CHOCOLATES
Valrhona-Chocolate.com

GUITTARD CHOCOLATE COMPANY
Guittard.com

GHIRARDELLI CHOCOLATE COMPANY
Ghirardelli.com

SCHARFFEN BERGER CHOCOLATE MAKER
Scharffenberger.com

EXTRACTS AND SYRUPS

TORANI
Torani.com

NIELSEN MASSEY FINE VANILLAS AND
FLAVORS
NielsenMassey.com

COOK'S
CooksVanilla.com

VANILLA BEAN KINGS
VanillaBeanKings.com

FLOURS AND SPECIALTY INGREDIENTS

KING ARTHUR FLOUR
shop.KingArthurFlour.com

BOB'S RED MILL
BobsRedMill.com

PASTURE-RAISED EGGS

VITAL FARMS
VitalFarms.com

Acknowledgments

To Emily for being my go-to for pie brainstorming and dilemmas. You've humored my chatter and ideas about baking for years and even stepped up to test recipes and share your experiences without tiring of my endless banter and nonlinear approach to problems. I appreciate your collaboration, friendship, and creative comradery.

To Kelsey for believing in this project from the start and helping mold a rough pie concept into this book. Your passion for baking and love of all things culinary and gorgeous cookbooks have given us so much to bond over.

To Lindsey for your stellar attention to detail and infinite patience with my tweaks, changes, questions, and worries. Your responsiveness, advice, and professionalism are so appreciated.

To Carrie, Robert, and Christy for your careful reading and for spotting inconsistencies and the many oversights that can happen on a project this size. I am thankful for your fine-comb considerations and adjustments.

To Chris for the day-to-day work you put into producing books. Thank you for always being willing to get that quote for whatever crazy printing effects I dream up. I am so grateful for everything you did to make this book a beautiful, printed piece.

To Brian for trusting me with the intricacies of the interior design and for all your advice and insight to make things flow correctly. Thank you for your collaboration and technical wisdom and for your hands-on efforts to bring this book design to the finish line.

To Olivia and the entire BPG marketing team for your care in bringing books to life from packaging to advertising to social media. Your know-how and passion for books has made working with you a joy.

To the BPG sales and publicity teams for all your behind-the-scenes work that goes into getting a book noticed and on shelves so it can find its way into the homes and hearts of readers.

To Will for allowing me to interrupt a ridiculously busy schedule to get help when I became stuck in the cover design process. Your visual brilliance is beyond compare. I'm so fortunate to have had your aid but even more lucky to have gotten to know and work with you.

To Jorge and Sancoy for bananas, gardenias, hibiscus, lady's slipper vine, tropical milkweed, coconuts, pineapples, mangos still on the branch, and lime boughs with tiny white flowers. Your ability to produce color, sustenance, and sweetness from the earth is commendable. I'm so grateful for the gathering of botanical props to grace my photography table.

To Kathy, who is like family, for teaching me all you know about from-scratch pumpkin pie; I appreciate the delight you take in all your creations and your years of making beautiful things grow.

To Rockelle for decades of friendship, good times, and hearty laughs. Thank you for sharing your holiday stories, and of course thanks also to your mom, Pennie, for her sweet potato pie.

To Brianna for the Carmelita inspiration and for sharing your relatable family baking traditions.

To Mumtaz for first telling me about nankhatai and encouraging me to add South Asian flavors to my baking roster. I appreciate the help with the proper spice balance for my Samosa Pie and your idea for the Pistachio and Rose Tart. Thank you for years of party planning, photography, design, and food styling collaboration. I wouldn't be who I am today without you and can't imagine life without your radiance, laughter, and grit.

To Dominga for teaching me traditional Guatemalan cooking methods from a lifetime of making meals for family and running your own *comedore*.

To Renee, Shannon, Megan, Betsy, Stacey, Allison, Carol, Paula, Laura, Michelle, and both of my Amy pals for all the support and love. You've celebrated and championed my work and been there for me with advice, taste-testing, and, best of all, conversation around delicious food.

To my kiddo and future baker, Leo. I can't tell you how much I love seeing you with a scoop of cake flour in one hand and the other on the controls of our stand mixer.

To my nieces, Victoria and Yoselin, for enduring kitchen chaos and helping me dig through the mess of nearly daily pie baking. I'm sure some pie marathons made you question my sanity, but you stayed calm and helped me carry on.

To Victor who confidently contradicted me every time I said that I couldn't do it.

Finally, to the littles, Gustavo and Beto, who fill the house with sound and life and wear on their faces the sweet evidence of thoroughly enjoyed pies.

Index

About the Author

LAURA KLYNSTRA is senior art director for Revell Books and a freelance graphic designer and photographer. Previously she worked as art director at Hyperion Books and at HarperCollins Publishers in New York City. She is the coauthor and photographer of *Christmas Baking* and *Gather & Graze*. She lives in Michigan with her family and a menagerie of dogs, cats, chickens, and ducks.

@SpiceAndSugarTable